I0540080

Dear Black Woman:

Honoring Our Inner Child with Love, Compassion, & Triumph

Volume 1

CO -AUTHORS

Loren A.
Simon

Mauryunna
Brown

Ann-Marie
Maloney

Nikki Shantell

Eternity Sledge

Zakiyyah
Broadnax

Mika
Newton

Meisha Pon

Robin
Blue

Dr. Kim
Manning

Brandi
Rhoden

Charleeta
Latham

Dr. Andrea
"Angel"
Taylor

Dear Black Woman:

Honoring Our Inner Child with Love, Compassion, & Triumph
Volume 1

Co-Authors: Ann Marie Maloney - Dr. Andrea "Angel" Taylor - Brandi Rohen - Charleeta Latham - Eternity Sledge - Dr. Kim Manning - Loren Simon - Mauryunna Brown - Meisha Pon - Mika Dean Newton - Nikki Shantell - Robin Blue - Zakiyyah Broadnax

Edited by Kami Redd & Co Branding, LLC
Published by REDD Ladys Publishing & Productions, LLC

Dedicated

To the girls we were and the women we are—the Black girls who became Black women and kept going.
To the child who needed safety and the woman who chose herself.
To those who stayed, those who left, and those still deciding.
To the ones who speak and the ones still finding words.
To the people who listened, and to the mothers, daughters, aunties, mentors, and friends who held us up.
For every survivor and every voice that now speaks: we see you, we honor you. This collection is yours.

"Asking for help makes you human."
– Meisha Pon

"Understand that your voice is your power, even if it trembles."
- Robin Blue

"You didn't lose your way. You made your way."
– Dr. Andrea "Angel" Atkinson-Taylor

Table of Contents

Foreword

Dear Black Woman,

When I first began writing *Dear Black Woman: Letters of Love, Strength, & Empowerment*, I did not know that I was planting the seed for something far larger than myself. At the time, I only knew pain. I knew what it felt like to carry childhood wounds that shaped the way I saw myself as an adult. I knew what it meant to smile on the outside while silently struggling inside. I knew what it felt like to be strong for everyone else yet still feel small, unseen, and unheard within.

Those first letters were meant for me alone. They were love notes to the little girl inside who never received the tenderness she deserved. They were written to comfort her, to remind her that she mattered, and to let her know that despite the chaos of the present, she was not forgotten. Each time I put pen to paper, I began to feel pieces of myself return—pieces I thought had been lost forever to shame, trauma, and silence.

What I did not realize then was that healing the inner child is not optional if we want to live fully. The little girl we once were does not disappear when we grow up; she lives inside our decisions, our relationships, our fears, and our hopes. If she was abandoned, she may show up in adulthood as mistrust. If she was silenced, she may appear as self-doubt. If she was shamed, she may linger as guilt we carry long after the moment has passed.

Writing those letters gave me a way to sit with her. It forced me to pause and ask her what she needed, what she missed, what she was still waiting to receive. In answering those questions, I began to realize something important: the healing we refuse in childhood becomes the burden we carry in adulthood. And unless we confront it, we pass that weight forward—to our children, to our partners, to our communities.

Childhood Wounds and the Present Moment

One of the greatest lessons I have learned is that unhealed childhood wounds steal the present from us. They drag us back into yesterday, replaying old hurts in new situations. They whisper lies into our ears—*You are not enough, you are too much, you are unworthy of love.* They dictate our choices before we even realize what we are doing.

For me, healing meant telling the truth about where the pain started. It meant looking at myself not as a woman who had failed, but as a child who had survived. That shift was everything. It allowed me to move away from judgment and toward compassion.

And yet, healing is not just about looking back. It is also about learning how to live here, in this moment. Too often, I found myself dwelling on the past or fearing the future. Healing invited me to release both. To breathe. To eat a meal and actually taste it. To laugh without worrying who might disapprove. To love without holding back pieces of myself in case rejection came again.

Living in the present moment is the gift of healing. It is where joy actually lives. Not in what was or what may be—but in now.

The Birth of This Anthology

As I continued my journey, I realized my story was only one among millions. I began to wonder what it would mean for other women to write their letters, too—to their younger selves, to their inner child, or to another Black woman who needed to hear her truth. That wondering turned into an invitation.

And to my amazement, women said yes.

Each co-author who joined this project brought courage with her. Courage to write openly. Courage to revisit painful moments. Courage to honor the child inside of her while also extending hope to others. These women did not come with polished, perfect stories, they came with real stories. Stories that bleed and heal, stories that ache and rise, stories that remind us that survival is never the end of the story.

Getting to know these women has been one of the greatest honors of my life. Through our conversations, I witnessed not just the writing of letters but the building of trust. I saw women holding space for each other across miles and time zones. I saw compassion extended when words failed and support offered when memories weighed too heavy.

In many ways, this anthology became a mirror of what community should be—each woman's story distinct, yet all of them woven together into a fabric strong enough to hold us all.

A Thank You to the Women Who Said Yes

To my co-authors: thank you.

Thank you for choosing honesty over silence. Thank you for pouring yourselves onto these pages, not for applause but for healing. Thank you for writing not only for yourselves but for the women who will read your words and realize they are not alone.

Your bravery has reminded me that healing is not something we do in isolation. It is a shared act, a collective decision to face what hurt us and to reclaim what was stolen. You have reminded me that sisterhood is not just an idea, it is a practice. It is found in the willingness to say, *"Here is my story. Here is my scar. Here is my song."*

Together, we have created a space where letters become bridges, carrying readers from pain to possibility, from silence to strength, from the past to the present.

To the Reader

As you hold this book in your hands, I ask you to read slowly. Breathe with the words. Allow yourself to feel what rises up. Some stories may mirror your own, others may feel far away, but each one carries a thread that ties us together.

If you find yourself crying, let the tears come. If you find yourself angry, sit with the anger. If you find yourself remembering moments you thought were long forgotten, honor them. This book is not meant to rush you; it is meant to meet you where you are.

And I hope you walk away with this truth: you are not your wounds. You are not your shame. You are not the mistakes others made with your life. You are whole. You are worthy. You are here—and the present moment is waiting for you to live it fully.

Moving Forward

This anthology is not an ending. It is the beginning. It is an invitation for you to pick up the pen and write your own letter—to the girl you once were, to the woman you are today, or to the Black woman you will become. It is a call to heal the wounds of childhood, not because the past can be undone, but because the present deserves all of you.

And as you do, remember: *Healing is a journey.*

Some days it will feel like progress, other days like standing still. But every honest step counts. Every moment of truth is a victory. Every word spoken in love is an act of liberation.

I began with letters to myself. This book ends with letters from many. May it continue with letters from you.

With love, gratitude, and hope,
Kami Redd

You

Become

By Dr. Andrea "Angel" Taylor

Dear Girl Who Carried Too Much, Too Soon,

You're seventeen and just starting to feel yourself.
Your hair is laid, your lip gloss is poppin', your jeans
are sitting just right, and you're walking through the
hallways of high school thinking, "Yeah… I look
good." You don't have a care in the world, just plans:
senior year, prom, the senior trip, graduation photos.
You think you've got time, and that the world will
wait for you to decide what's next.

And then, everything changes.

One test. Two lines. One life, growing inside your
own. You stare at that test for what feels like hours.
Your hands shake. Your chest tightens. You aren't
sure if you want to scream, cry, or disappear. And
just like that, it hits you: you're pregnant.

And before you even tell a soul, the shame sets in.
Not because of the baby, but because of the silence
you already know is coming. Because deep down,
you know you can't tell them. Not yet. Not your
parents. Not your brothers. Not your role model
cousin in Chicago. Not the people who raised you
with dreams and expectations, who brought you

from Jamaica, W.I., to America for a better life. How do you tell them that life just got… complicated?

So, you hide it.

Oversized hoodies. Strategically timed bathroom breaks. Avoiding too much eye contact. You move through the world like a ghost—present, but unseen. You carry a secret that gets heavier every day. You even keep it from your parents, too ashamed to explain what you couldn't fully understand. You still pretend to get your period, changing pads even though there's no blood. And still, you show up. You do your homework. You laugh on cue. You pretend you're okay.

But you are not okay.

You are seventeen and suffocating, living two lives. One in public, where you're still a girl. One in private, where you're already somebody's mother. And when you finally say it out loud, "I'm pregnant," it doesn't feel brave. It feels like you're breaking, like every part of your childhood falls away in a single breath. Their disappointment hurts more than anything your body has been through. And even though you understand it, that doesn't make it easier. You missed prom. You missed your senior trip. You missed the carefree parts of being young because now, everything is real. There's no turning back.

But baby girl… you make it.

You push through.

You give birth and graduate in the same breath. You walk across that stage with your cap and gown, not just for yourself, but for her, the little girl who would grow up watching you become more than what people expected. They counted you out. You counted yourself back in. You didn't let shame define you; you let it sharpen you. And somehow, in the middle of all of that… you got chosen.

Fresh out of high school, you stepped into a world that didn't slow down for anyone. You walked into that downtown office building at J.P. Morgan on Wall Street, still barely out of school, and took your place in the corporate trust department. You were one of the few chosen. While others your age were still finding their footing, you were creating stocks and bonds, processing paperwork, thinking faster than the pace of the city around you. No roadmap, just your will. You sat at desks not designed for girls like you, and still, you left your mark.

You didn't get there by luck. You built your way there.

Still, even then, you knew this wasn't your final stop. There was more ahead. More to give. More to become.

So, you pivoted.

When your daughter was ten, you became a Licensed Practical Nurse. You balanced work and motherhood with quiet determination. When she turned fourteen, you did the unthinkable again: you went back to school. First for your RN, then your BSN—something many dream of, but few finish while raising a family. You studied by day, worked night shifts, and still made time for care, community, and compassion. You showed up for patients with your whole heart because you understood what it meant to persevere. Your patients didn't just get a nurse; they got a woman who knew how to survive and still serve.

You could've stopped there. Could've built a good, respectable life and called it enough. But that's not who you are. You kept building. You kept becoming.

Now look at you.

A mother of three: your firstborn daughter and two beautiful sons. A wife, again—this time, wiser. Not because you regret the first marriage, but because you grew from it. That union was built on love. It didn't last, but it helped you find yourself. There is no bitterness, only gratitude. Now, love looks different. It isn't love finally arriving; its love unfolding. Not because it was missing, but because you've evolved. Now, you experience it with clarity, peace, and joy.

And that's not all.

You're a co-owner of an entertainment company, bringing joy, rhythm, and celebration to others. You know how to create moments that matter. That's always been your gift. You're also a nurse, administering infusions to immunocompromised patients, showing up with compassion and care. You're the founder of Nourish then Flourish Collective, a nonprofit built to help people balance mind, body, and spirit—to pause, grow, bloom, and thrive. You created a space for others to come home to themselves because you remember what it felt like to disappear. You're an ambassador for Queen City Women in Business / ProcuraFind®. You're the voice behind Color Me In Sound, a podcast for Black women creatives who are tired of hiding their brilliance. You remind us we don't need permission to take up space; we already belong. You're the Chapter President of Dear Black Woman – North Carolina, leading, uplifting, and listening. You mentor women through Nasdaq Milestone Circles, helping them scale their businesses and believe in themselves, because your reach isn't bound by geography. You do it because you remember. You remember being seventeen. You remember hiding. You remember shame. You remember silence. And you vowed: no Black woman should ever have to walk that alone if you can help it.

And then… there's her.

Your daughter. The same baby you once held with trembling hands and silent tears. Now? She's a CRNA—a Certified Registered Nurse Anesthetist, with a master's degree in nursing. A world traveler. She walks with confidence and purpose. She laughs loudly. Loves freely. Lives boldly.

And you did that.

You didn't just raise her; you raised a legacy. You didn't just raise children; you raised generations. Your sons? They are strength. They are possibility. They are purpose. And they will know how to honor women. They will know how to build and protect love. Because you showed them. You did not fail them. You gave them you.

So, if I could sit next to you at seventeen, hold your hand, and whisper just one thing in your ear, it would be this:

You become.

YOU: The girl who cried in silence.

YOU: The girl who thought she ruined everything.

YOU: The girl who hated her reflection for a while.

YOU: The girl who felt invisible, unworthy, and unready...

YOU BECOME:

A Mother.

A Wife.

A Trusted Confidant.

A Businesswoman.

A Nurse.

A Founder.

A Leader.

A Mentor.

A Visionary.

A Force.

Most of all, a woman who does not just survive, but teaches others how to thrive.

You didn't lose your way. You made your way.

And baby girl…

Look at you now.

With love and resilience,
Andrea "Angel" Atkinson-Taylor, BSN, RN

Beloved

By Ann Marie Maloney

Dear Black Woman,

I am so glad that you've learned to rest in the center of your soul.

In a world that often demands you to be everything to everyone, it's a radical act to prioritize your own peace and well-being. Annie, you navigated through a maze of expectations, stereotypes, and trials that you believed to have crushed you. Until you realized the lie for what it is. "Hard pressed on every side but not crushed; perplexed but not abandoned; struck down but not destroyed." - 2 Corinthians 4:8-9.

Annie, here you are still standing even after you were left bewildered – left behind like trash put out on the curb.

How did you get here? How did we get here?

How did we lose so much of ourselves that I would abandon you to chase someone who couldn't love me?

I am a different woman now, and this letter is what I want to tell you. Take my hand and let's talk.

Remember when you were about 10? On one occasion, you asked Mommy how she burned her arm. She said it was an accident, but she knew, and I knew in my soul that it wasn't an accident. I reached to comfort her, but she shooed me away, dismissing her pain. She couldn't tell, and I didn't have the words. I was a child. But I felt her in me.

It would be years before I knew this was not a betrayal; but her own quiet strength covering her truth. It would be years before I had the maturity to grasp this; years where I unlearned to dismiss myself. I was a child, and I felt my mommy in me. Her pain became mine; her way of dealing with it became mine too.

Daddy bounced you on his lap, nicknamed you Baby Girl, even promising you a bicycle. You waited for weeks, staring out the front window waiting for him to come home from work. He came home from work, but no bicycle with him. Annoyed, he accused you of making the whole thing up. Baby Girl, you learned to accept that people will misrepresent you, so how could you trust yourself? How can you believe anybody else's promises?

I grew to understand the rhythms of childhood – parents are perfectly imperfect. Their actions stem from their own struggles that were never our burden to carry.

Baby Girl, since you put your water pots down, don't you feel yourself becoming lighter? By accepting their infallibility, you are part of the puzzle that allows them to be free. I'm proud of you for honoring the ways in which both parents walk with you in Spirit with a pure heart.

Do you remember the 1st boy you kissed? He was the cutest boy in middle school. Like girls my age, I had this fantasy of what it would be like to be kissed by a boy. Not like what you think. A bookworm, a nerd, teased by classmates for wearing glasses, for my family's accent, for my homemade clothes and braided hair, and he picked me. Oh, how my heart fluttered when he asked. I said yes.

The kiss was sweet. It was gentle. It was soft. He let me go and hurried away.

I floated into the classroom to tell my best friend. All eyes on me, before everyone started laughing. He won the bet that he would kiss the ugliest girl in the school.

I was the bet.

Oh, how you and I dreamt, fell in love, and played with imaginary friends in stories and plays. Wasn't it fun to read about love from Jane Austen or solve mysteries as Agatha Christie spun her yarn? Whatever drew you, I wonder, to Homer's "Iliad," Cervantes' "Catcher in the Rye" or Lewis' version of "The Aeneid of Virgil?" You didn't know what it all meant. How could you know then, that when sisters and brothers left home to find their own path, that books would be the covering that the Almighty gave you.

The construct of being alone bound you with cords of depression. You felt abandoned, forgotten, and left behind. Mommy worked double shifts to pay the mortgage; daddy was gone too, leaving no one but you. You fed yourself, clothed yourself, and put yourself to bed. It is a wound so deep I felt it too–in you and in the grown up me.

What's also true, when taken from a different perspective, you were protected.

No partying. No pregnancies. No STDs. No skirmishes with the law. The shield of your naivete enabled you to start college at 16, one of your crowning achievements. The year at the predominantly white university was out of alignment with your being. But "Oh Howard, I sing of thee." There was a whole other world written by Langston Hughes, Lorraine Hanesberry, Zora Neale Hurston, August Wilson, and Chinua Achebe when you matriculated at the mecca – Howard University.

For every "A" you earned, you were still worried.

"Am I good enough?"

"Am I pretty enough?"

"Is Greek life for me? Student government, perhaps?"

Always on the outside looking in, trying to fit in. Who was it that instilled in you, or me when I was you, to keep your legs closed? There were no mother-daughter talks or auntie tea parties. I don't know, I just knew it in my spirit to do so.

And because you Baby Girl couldn't grasp the paradox of wanting the attention of a boyfriend, and being afraid to put out, as college students so frequently do, I let go of your hand. We disconnected - I lost you and I lost me. When the girls flirted and left with dates at the party, without so much as a goodbye, you stopped being sweet. Standing in a stranger's house, house party music jamming, young adults grinding in corners with no light, stricken with fear.

But God. The boy who walked me to my dorm room after midnight did not harm me. Then again boys wouldn't have seen me in that way because of how many times I failed their F.A.T. test (face-ass-titties). Dazed and confused, Annie, you and I persevered – separately.

"I should have known better," I tell myself like so many women do.

This is a lie.

"How was I supposed to know better? Who stepped in the gap to teach me and answer the questions I didn't know to ask?"

Baby Girl for all the years we lost touch with one another, I did not know about self-worth and value. I did not learn about boundaries and red flags. I did not know how to protect you because I didn't see you. I was too busy trying to survive. So, when he asked me out, I surrendered. His personality became our identity, and you and I disappeared completely.

In their migration patterns, salmon swim upstream, against the current. When you feel like a nobody, it may seem that you're drifting. That's a lie. In actuality, like salmon swimming upstream, the work is twice as hard. You're pushing, you're grinding, but you're moving in circles. People pleasing and imposter syndrome is born in the current of adversity. One looks for love, everywhere but inside. Every now and then, you find fool's gold.

I walked out after midnight. (Why does everything happen at midnight)? Dragging a small suitcase, mostly toiletries and one change of clothing, I thrust it in the car seat beside me and stepped on the gas.

It was already dark, and I could not see. The misty rain outside fogged up the windshield and the tears rolled down my cheeks fogged up the inside. No plan. No friends. I would want to wake up in the middle of the night.

I pulled into the hotel parking lot; the same one I had gone to many times for meetings and conferences for work. The next morning, I checked out of the hotel and even went to work, like it was normal. When work was over, I sat in the car with nowhere to go. I would rather die before I spent another day being shamed, insulted, and humiliated.

"That didn't happen, and if it did, it wasn't that bad, and if it was, it's not a big deal, and if it is, it's not my fault and if it was, I didn't mean it, and if I did, you made me do it." - Anonymous.

Baby Girl, you saved me. Your belief of what love should be finally breaking through – this sh** ain't normal.

In 30 years, I existed in unhealthy patterns. No need to speak them, less it draws energy to itself.

"Where would I live?"

"How will I pay for housing?"

"What about my children?"

I locked myself in a prison pondering these questions. I never rested. That day, I saw your reflection in the mirror. I was my own jailer. A man's actions stem from his own struggles. I was wise enough not to try to change him, foolish enough to want to help him. As a woman, society teaches us to carry our own burdens, and his too. Peering into the mirror, my spirit said, "no mas." "No more." It's not mine to carry.

Walking out at midnight is not scary when you understand that dawn comes in the morning. I found myself in every broken piece, and I called you Baby Girl back to myself. But God. "Whoever dwells in the shelter of the Most High will rest in the shadow of the Almighty. I will say of the Lord, "He is my refuge and my fortress, my God in whom I trust…You will not fear the terror of night, nor the arrow that flies by day, nor the pestilence that stalks in the darkness, nor the plague that destroys at midday." (Psalm 91: 1-2, 5-6)

Mommy, the woman who hid her pain, paid the lawyer's retainer fee. I slept on the floor of an apartment until a church donor bought over a couch. (My back still hurts). My sister-friend bought me dishes. My auntie, who transitioned to glory, left me an inheritance. I own a home because of her. Glory! This is how you emerge from the fire – women gather and move in silence.

Still, I carry too many water pots. Children are both our greatest joy and our most profound responsibility. In the face of their needs, I forget to nurture myself. Or did I? Baby Girl, I gave them my all, never stopping to think you needed me and I needed you too.

I thought a woman was supposed to pour our love, energy, and resources into our children. In this noble task, some of us neglect our own identities. I wish someone would have told me to save a little for myself. But the truth is, I would not have listened.

39

Truth be told, longsuffering will keep you discouraged. My love for them is the reason I got out of bed. They were my reason for waking up. Unfair, perhaps? But survival by any means necessary.

So many others understood self-care long before it was an idea for me. Though self-care and motherhood seem to be on opposite ends of the spectrum, it's a choice. A better choice is to flow wherever joy takes you while balancing one's responsibility. It's a delicate dance – one that brings life to both. And now, you and I are free to dance with childlike wonder.

Pieces of you came back in God winks. Baby Girl, your light broke through when I started riding my bike. Oh, how you laughed. Hiking, walking, water aerobics and strength conditioning would come and go. These were holistic remedies softening the blow of aging, all the while doing things you missed as a child.

I saw you again when I ventured out with my sister friend in adventures that didn't seem possible for me. Then you had the audacity to fly domestic and

40

international trips – solo and in groups. You brought playfulness to my job and changed its toxic patterns to joy.

God winked again when I shepherded my students to shine on various stages – doing it in a way that I wish someone had done for you.

God winked when I started coaching Spoken Word - you showed up when I took the stage myself.

God winked when I started the About This Life podcast - and our voice became amplified.

God winked when I chose to start writing again – something you were doing when you scribbled in marble notebooks at 3 years old.

What I know now that I didn't know then was that I was calling the little girl back to myself.

Your joy tempered with setbacks. Being a woman is not a simple life. We wrestle with being objectified or labeled as angry.

If you don't speak up, you're too timid.

If you stand 10 toes down, you are an angry Black woman.

If you put up steel around your heart, love can't flow in or out.

If you open with softness, you are seen as weak.

If you reveal your intelligence, you're too worldly.

If you admit to not knowing the latest sports news, you're dismissed as irrelevant.

If you dress conservatively, you remind potential suitors of their mother.

If you dress curvaceously, you attract fleas.

If you have standards, you're too inflexible.

If you let them down, you're too easy.

If you wear weaves, you're fake.

If you allow premature gray to take up residence, you're too old.

Being a strong Black woman is not child's play. The mental acuity and discernment needed to peer into the motives of others is quite simply exhausting. Sometimes you get it right, sometimes you don't. Baby Girl, this older version of you just wanted to lay down her crown.

And so, you did. That night at the concert, standing, to catch the last few musical notes, he held me. My body, without so much as a thought, surrendered. Whatever neuroscience-y language applies, my body dropped as a wave of negative energy left. His arms encircling me, I fell back onto his chest behind me, keeping me from falling to the ground. First time in my life I felt safe.

Safe to be myself.

Safe to make mistakes.

Safe to share my secrets.

Safe to share my dreams.

Safe to exhale.

Safe.

Until I was left bewildered standing on a curb.

When a lover leaves, we carry their shadows and a torrent of questions:

"Did I not love you enough?"

"Was I not worthy of being cherished?"

"Did I not listen to your stories and your songs long enough?"

"Did I not lift you up and support your decisions enough?"

"Did I not speak tender mercies to the war-torn places of your heart?"

"Did I not offer you my lap to hold the weariness in your shoulders?"

Baby Girl, you are more than a conqueror.

Let them go – the questions and the lover.

You already know Baby Girl, the wound is not the end of our story: it's just a chapter.

Once you release the need to know all the answers, the need for "closure," I promise you, the churning stops. In the by and by, when you know that you know that you know, it's come to this – you little girl is whom I shall love first. I am my own first love. In gathering all the pieces of you back home to myself, lays the path to becoming enough.

You're looking at me to see if I'm different. Wondering if you can trust the woman. I am not perfect, but I will do better. I found the key to unlock the pattern. It's you. I see you. I will make mistakes, but I will not betray you again. I will be the adult in the room that you always needed. You will be my reminder to laugh, to play, to dance.

"I reclaim my narrative and yours too."

"You have a light inside you that cannot be extinguished."

"No matter what others say, you are magic."

"You are beautiful."

"You are worthy of more."

"You deserve more."

"I will look for the good in every day."

"I release regret and expectations. I accept that I can miss someone and still send love and light especially on days when it makes no sense. This path leads to embodying – love."

"I surrender to stillness, letting my body rest from the overstimulation of world affairs, work, and so on."

"I listen to the rain and allow it to taste my tears knowing that the sun will come again."

"I rest from the tyranny of my triggers by asking Baby Girl where it hurts? I trace pain to its source, change the limiting belief, and I free you."

"I will dance because Mommy loved to dance. So what if you giggle? Mommy giggled like a schoolgirl all the time."

"I will wear my hats because Daddy loved his fedora."

"I take my medicine: I walk in the sunlight. I dance. I write. I coach. I share. I pray."

"I cease striving and rest because all the pieces of myself returned, and I am whole."

And as Isaiah 61:1-7 proclaims,

"The Spirit of the Sovereign Lord is on me,

because the Lord has anointed me

to proclaim good news to the poor.

He has sent me to bind up the brokenhearted,

to proclaim freedom for the captives

and release from darkness for the prisoners,

to proclaim the year of the Lord's favor

and the day of vengeance of our God,

to comfort all who mourn

and provide for those who grieve in Zion –

to bestow on them a crown of beauty

instead of ashes,

the oil of joy

instead of mourning,

and a garment of praise

instead of a spirit of despair.

They will be called oaks of righteousness,

a planting of the Lord

for the display of his splendor.

They will rebuild the ancient ruins

And restore the places long devastated;

they will renew the ruined cities

that have been devastated for generations.

Strangers will shepherd your flocks;

foreigners will work your fields and vineyards,

And you will be called priests of the Lord,

You will be named ministers of our God.

You will feed on the wealth of nations,

and in their riches, you will boast

Instead of your shame

you will receive a double portion,

and instead of disgrace

you will rejoice in your inheritance.

And so, you will inherit a double portion in your land,

and everlasting joy will be yours."

I leave you with this gift -

This space holds both grief and gold.

I am not what was done to me.

I am what rose from it.

I am your Beloved.

You are my Baby Girl.

Yes, and Amen ~

The Girl I Carried, The Woman I Became

By Brandi Rohen

Dear Little Black Girl,

I see you. I hear you. I sit with you. I care for you. I mourn with you. I cheer for you. I love you.

Since I came to know you, I've always recognized that you were much stronger than the average child. A child who had to grow up much too fast. A child who only got to experience pure, innocent joy for only a fleeting period of time. A child who was silenced by being indoctrinated to stay in a child's place.

And yet, even then, I admired you. I admired your bravery, your courage to hold secrets that no child should ever be responsible to carry. I admired the way you smiled in photos, even though you often felt alone in the room. The way you helped others without ever being asked. The way you could read the energy of a room the moment you walked in, scanning for safety as if this was a familiar practice for you. You were intuitive before you had language to describe what that meant. You were resilient before you even knew the word.

Dear Black Woman, I watched you learn to survive only receiving guidance that "it won't be like this always," to make sense of chaos with the emotional tools of a child. And still you showed up. You didn't ask for this strength you were forced to carry, but you did it anyway. With grace. With confusion. And at times, with fear. You didn't ask for the wounds, but you tried to turn them into wisdom. You didn't ask to grow up in survival mode, but you adapted, beautifully and painfully, like a flower growing through concrete.

This letter is for you—not just the woman you've become, but the girl you once were. The one who kept showing up, sometimes with nothing to give, but kept showing up, kept trying, kept hoping. The one who learned far too early that love doesn't always look like safety and security. This chapter is your reminder that you deserved so much more, and you are still worthy of everything good. You always have been.

Before I continue, I want to offer you care in the form of a pause and to serve as a potential trigger warning.

Dear Black Woman reading this who resonates with my story, you deserve to be witnessed gently. Before I unfold the next part of my story, I want to hold your heart with care. What I'm about to share includes details of childhood trauma, including sexual abuse, traumatic loss, and domestic violence. I share this not to reopen wounds, but to name what was once unspeakable—to give voice to the little girl in me who couldn't speak for herself. This section is not meant to shock the world, but to liberate you. To give you the power back that was once stripped from you. If you need to take a moment, please do. Your well-being matters. This part of my story isn't meant to cause harm, but to hold space for truth—my truth—and to show that healing is possible, even from the places we once thought would destroy us. Some of what is shared may be heavy. Though I won't force every memory into the light, I may offer pieces of the truth that you are willing to share with the world. You deserve to be heard. This is owed to you, the little girl who waited for someone to see her pain and call it what it was. I offer this part of my story with compassion, not only for myself, but for anyone else who is still learning how to name their own pain and call it what it is.

So here it is—what I remember, what I felt, and what I carried. I write this not just to look back, but to make peace with the parts of my story that shaped me before I had the words to claim them. This is where the silence ends, and the remembering begins.

You learned quickly that you were to be seen and not heard. Somewhere along the way, you began to believe your voice was not meant to take up space, not knowing this would cause you to struggle with speaking up for yourself and getting your needs met while being so loud advocating for everyone else later on in life. My first encounter of advocating for others wasn't once I became a social worker, but as a tender child, calling my mother's mother, grandmother, to save her from the violence, the unhappiness, the toxicity, and most of all to save me.

I know you don't remember much before the age of ten—and what you do recall felt like a blur of noise and absence. The details are scattered, like puzzle pieces you've never quite been able to put together. I know something shifted in you long before you were ready. Somewhere after the age of five, you stopped feeling like a child and started simply existing. Your mother worked often, and your father lived hours away with his new family. You spent a lot of time with my grandparents, being cared for the best everyone knew how. Home was not always a safe place.

Though you never saw the fists flying, you heard the yelling. The pleading. The crying. You heard the fear in her voice when she thought you were asleep, sometimes not asleep in the middle of the day. You heard the sharpness in his. That kind of environment teaches you to be small, to be still, to listen for danger in silence. And somewhere in the shadows of those years, something was taken from you that you didn't fully understand—but you felt the weight of it all the same.

Maybe you didn't have the words back then, but your body remembered. The tightening in your throat, trying to hold back the tears. The questions behind your eyes. The ache of being seen only when you were being helpful. Even then, that was sometimes met with frustration because you were supposed to stay in a child's place and not share what went on in your household.

But what you were told to keep quiet about went beyond the yelling and fighting. There were other violations—ones that lived behind closed doors and in the shadows of your silence. Somewhere beginning after your fifth birthday, you experienced the touch of a man that wasn't supposed to happen. You didn't have the words then, but you knew something was wrong. You knew your body wasn't supposed to be touched. You knew the look in his eyes wasn't safe. You knew how it felt to freeze. To drift off into a land inside of your mind that would protect you and keep you safe until it was over. To pretend it didn't happen so you could make it through another day. And, now as an adult, I need you to know, Black Woman: that it was not your fault. What happened to you was abuse. You were a child. You didn't invite that into your life. You didn't imagine it. And you didn't deserve it. Speaking it aloud now isn't about reliving it. It's about freeing the part of you that still carries the shame, even though none of it belonged to you.

No one had a clue what was going on, except my father's mother, who suspected something was happening but didn't have all of the pieces to put together.

This sick pattern went on for years, only ending the night my mother was taken from my brother and me due to a tragic car accident. Your mother shared with you she was leaving and would be right back. I remember you asking her if you could leave and go with her to the store to gas up her small red Toyota Paseo for the week. At the door, she asked, "Has he been messing with you?" Frightened and caught off guard by her question and quickly remembering what he told me he would share about me if I ever told anyone what he was doing, "No," I replied. To this day, I often wonder if she knew that you were scared to stay with him or simply fed up with being violated. Did your eyes tell a story? Did you give off a vibe? Or did her motherly instinct tell something was wrong? You remember her saying, "Stay here and help with your brother," as she backed out of the driveway, knowing what was going to happen to you while she was gone. You don't remember what else she said to you before she left that day, what she wore, how she smelled, if she hugged you.

What I do remember is our neighbor from across the street, an older white man who must have been sitting and listening to the police scanner, knocking on the door, interrupting him, violating me. Something about the air seemed off after he shared with us that we'd better go down to the police station because there's been a bad accident near our home with a car that fit the description of hers. We go down to the police station, and the County coroner comes in with sadness and heartbreak in his eyes. My mother's boyfriend asks, "Please tell me she's okay." He drops his head and says something that is inaudible in my memory, but I recall you and him bursting into tears.

Time stood still after that. The silence in the police car on the ride to my grandparents' house where I broke the news to her father and brother that she was gone. One moment, I had a mother, and in the next, I was motherless.

Everything between ages five and ten is blurry, but that night is burned into you. You may not recall the days in full, but you remember the shift in the world. You remember feeling like something in you shut down, but like a sense of relief in the same breath

59

that it was finally over and you wouldn't be hurt anymore.

In reality, the hurting had really just begun. You didn't know that her death wouldn't just mean the loss of a parent—it would mean the loss of a protector, a sense of home, and the only person who ever halfway understood the chaos we lived through.

In the Black community, when a family member passes away, everyone congregates at that person's home or an immediate family member's home. I see you standing on the porch, looking out into traffic, trying to hide the pain. Still smiling when grieving family members walk up to hug you. Masking pain was a regular practice that you'd perfected by this point. You didn't know how to take up space. You didn't know how to have a voice to express yourself. You remember taking care of other family members who were close with your mother by hugging and consoling them, letting them know everything was going to be fine. At ten years old, you had the strength of a praying grandmother. Strength you probably shouldn't have had at that age.

In the days after she passed, going back to the house was hard. The air was so thick you could cut it with a knife, and the silence was so loud. The house felt empty. You felt empty.

If I could go back to speak to you, the little girl standing on that porch trying to be strong for everyone else—I wouldn't ask you to smile. I wouldn't ask you to be brave. I would kneel down, take your tiny hands in mine, and say, "You don't have to hold it all together. Not today. Not for them." I'd tell you it's okay to fall apart. That grief doesn't need to be quiet to be valid. That it was never your job to comfort grown people while your own heart was breaking. I would tell you that you are more than the strength you perform. Even though everything feels shattered now, your softness is not lost—it's just buried, waiting to be safe enough to rise again. I would let you cry. I would hold you until your shoulders stopped trembling. I would whisper, over and over again, "You didn't deserve any of this—but I promise you, one day, you'll reclaim every piece of yourself that was stolen. And you'll do it with love."

Little Black girl, I want to honor what you witnessed me go through throughout life and acknowledge the strength you had to embody that you didn't need to embody during those ages.

After it settled in that mama died, the days turned into weeks, and everything around you kept moving like nothing had happened. You learned early that the world doesn't pause for your pain. All of the grown folks around you kept saying, "She's in a better place," but no place felt better to you. You always felt there was something missing from your life, but yet you pressed on. You returned to school like normal, showed up like normal, and performed strength like normal—but you weren't okay, and you didn't even know that you weren't okay. You were grieving a mother, mourning a childhood, and burying emotions you didn't yet know how to name.

You remember trying to talk about her a few times, but in your primary household, the people around you didn't really want to hear your pain. Kids didn't have pain in their eyes. What is that? You had better pray and move on. I thank God that your father's mother was there for you, encouraging you along the way. "It won't be like this always, Brandi" is what she would tell you when you confided in her about the big emotions you were experiencing. She was the only one who, at the time, helped you realize it was okay to not be okay, but that wasn't enough for you.

Enough people didn't recognize your pain. They wanted resilience. They wanted you to be okay. So you became just what they needed—not because you were healed, but because being "strong" kept you from being a burden. You became the quiet helper. The achiever. The one everyone knew would make it out of that poor little town that you grew up in. The one who didn't cause trouble. The one your father often told, "I know I never have to worry about you," when in fact, he should've been worried about you the most. You became the one who kept it together.

Only on the surface.

But inside? You were still that ten-year-old little girl searching for safety. Wondering if anyone would ever come for you. Wishing someone could see through the smiles, the straight A's, the perfect performances, and ask, "Are you really okay?" The answer was no. And yet, you kept showing up.

There's something so isolating about grieving in silence. About being told you're so "mature for your age," you have an "old soul," or comments about your rapidly developing body, when really, you're just carrying more than any child ever should. You learned to numb. To stay busy. To start new projects and never finish them. To be so close to people, but so emotionally distant at the same time. Not because you didn't want love, but because that's actually all that you wanted, in the same breath remembering that "love" had already cost you so much.

Even in the years that followed, survival looked like high-functioning pain. Like showing up in spaces and making everyone comfortable, at the expense of your own comfort. Like excelling in school while feeling completely unseen. Like suppressing everything that made you feel too much, too soft, too loud, too human. Like working three and four jobs at a time to remain distracted from the world. To survive. To numb. Yet never resting or taking care of yourself. Never choosing you first.

But even then, little Black girl, you were worthy. You didn't need to earn that worth through performance or perfection. You always deserved to be held and to take up space, even in your mess. Even in your anger. Even in your "sensitivity." Even in your grief.

And even through all of that pain—through the loss, the violation, the silence, the pretending—baby girl, you built a life. Not a perfect one. Not one without setbacks, because you've had plenty of those. But a life that is yours.

You loved and were loved. You birthed joy into this world in the form of two beautiful, bright little boys—pieces of your heart walking this earth, reminding you daily of how much good you are capable of creating. You've raised them with tenderness and intention, giving them the kind of presence and protection you once longed for yourself.

You dared to dream beyond survival. You built businesses from the ground up—not just for profit, but for purpose. You turned your pain into passion and your trauma into tools that now help others find their way back to themselves. You've become a safe

65

space, not only for your clients and your community, but also yourself.

You reclaimed your voice. You learned how to rest, how to say no, how to soften without guilt and shame. You made space for healing. You made room for joy. You made a home within yourself, the kind of home you never had growing up. And you did all of this while still carrying that little girl inside you. She never left—but now, you've finally turned toward her. And that is the real victory. Not the degrees, not the titles, not the accolades. But the fact that you're still here when you've considered voluntary death many times. Whole. Healing. Choosing yourself, again and again.

Little Black girl, I deeply apologize to you that it took thirty years to realize you are the most important, most cherished possession in your life. I deeply apologize to you that it took thirty years to realize you need to rest to have the energy and capacity to keep moving forward. Little Black girl, I deeply apologize for abandoning you without getting to know you, not realizing I was operating out of the hurt that I'd felt all of my life. Abandoned. Little Black girl, I invite you to join me from this day forward to be a united force. I will forever honor you. I will forever meet your needs without putting you on the back burner or treating you as an afterthought. I will no longer ignore you.

To the Black Woman you've become, I see you. I hear you. I sit with you. I care for you. I celebrate your softness, your strength, your becoming. I cheer for your growth, your rest, your joy. And above all, I love you fully, deeply, without condition.

With All My Love,
Brandi (Me)

Breaking the Silence

By Charleeta Latham

I know nothing's been the same since the sun set. She was our sun, our moon, and our star. And that's a good thing. There were, well…are a lot of people who thought losing her would weaken (maybe even flat-out cripple) you and if we're being honest, there were times I would've believed those people were right. But I thank God Mama did for us the same thing her mother did for her. She taught us restraint and embodied divinity. She showed us the beauty in our reflection long before anyone else had an opinion.

I know who I am, and I know my heavenly Father's voice. (You do, too.) So, this world's projections, lies, and manipulation fail at every turn. Of course, I don't listen because if you don't speak to me the way God does, you're not talking to or about me. There's no way anyone could be.

She used to say if her mother hadn't been so intentional about building her confidence and grounding her in her identity when she was a little girl, she wouldn't have had any. Now, she didn't say this part but, in my mind, Grandma knew she wouldn't be with her long. So, she was sure to give her what she needed to live without her before she had to go.

It wasn't until shortly before Mama's passing that I learned that it had always been a fear of hers that she would have to leave you before you were ready to be without her. Hearing that brought the flood because before that moment, I'd never considered her fear.

You've never been afraid of much, but you've always been fearful of losing her. Just the thought of life without her has caused you to spiral.

We share a face, mannerisms, and vocal tone. Never had I imagined that we also shared a fear. She was afraid of leaving me and I was afraid of being left behind.

The way Mama faced life made me wonder if she ever had been fearful of anything at all. And I've always made it a personal practice to face what scares me (well except bees, we're still working on that one lol). It's been four years since we had no choice but to face our greatest fear and keep living.

Watching Mama hang on just for you will shift something in your spirit. It may even be safe to say that it will awaken something in you. There will be times when you will hate it here without her. Mama was our sun, our moon, and our star.

But look at you. Look at me. Look at us! You always knew. You called it. You stayed and you held on to the vision. Now, look at us. This is just as much because of you as it is because of me. I would not be standing here on the other side of all the neglect, betrayal, mistreatment, and abuse if you had not been so determined. Your quiet defiance saved our life. You refused to let go and look at us now. Living our dream and loving our life.

Uncle Ed used to randomly tell you how you were anointed all the time. More specifically, he would say your hands were anointed. I don't think I fully appreciated him seeing me until I was well into adulthood.

When I think back about my experience of the other adults in my life during that time, I remember being met with judgment or loud silence. It was almost as if acknowledging something positive (or anything

that didn't justify harsh punishment) was against
their religion.

I remember them frequently striking my boisterous
cousin in the mouth for seemingly just being a child.
It felt to me as though they were trying to break her
spirit. She was always loud, happy, and joyful. Her
hysterical laughter could break the sound barrier.
She has one of those contagious laughs. You don't
even have to know what she's laughing at. Well, I
didn't.

I remember hearing/overhearing them compare us.
In contrast, you were the "quiet" one. I remember
somebody saying, "Why can't you be more like your
cousin?" or something to that effect basically
suggesting that I was different or better because I
was quieter…milder…easier to miss…

You were not then, nor have you ever been quiet.
You just didn't want to get your teeth knocked down
your throat for simply laughing or, God forbid, being
a happy, joyful child.

Fear of judgment will make you do things so
differently. I wouldn't realize the ways in which I

was shrinking and censoring myself until I was well into adulthood. But in the meantime, I would find myself trying to "run block" for her. Thinking I was doing her a favor, I would try to catch her before they did. If I noticed her getting too loud or if I noticed them noticing her, I'd try to distract them or calm her down myself.

It would take me too long to realize I wasn't doing either one of us a favor. While I understand they were doing what they believed to be best (as I choose to believe most of us are), the impact of this family dynamic would set off a ripple effect that would ultimately lead you to choose emotional detachment and physical distance.

For years, you observed from (what felt like) afar. You watched your father judge and belittle your older siblings when they came to him for help. So, you learned never to do that. You never asked. Even though you would need it, you never asked for it. You never wanted to be spoken to (or about) in the ways you heard your siblings spoken to. So, you just did without it. They praised you for this, but it never felt good.

You were an "easy" child because you learned early on how to quietly channel your chaotic, childish energy into more acceptable behavioral patterns and creative endeavors, essentially hiding in plain sight. Standing in the middle of the room while feeling completely invisible must have been incredibly disorienting and I'm sorry you had to experience that.

You were never quiet. You are and always have been just as loud. Just as boisterous. Just as hard to miss.

But they did. They missed me. Your father says things like, "I told so and so. My daughter don't ask me for nothing! She don't give me no problems."

And they say things like, "We never had to worry about you." Well, maybe they should have. But I need you to know this. Feel it. Understand it and get it deep down into your being. Maybe they were simply doing the best they could or maybe they were simply negligent. It doesn't matter. You have me and I've got you.

There was never anything wrong with you. Their failings were never about you. They were not a reflection of you. Listen to me carefully. I did not say you were never wrong. What I said was, there was never anything wrong WITH YOU. You were a child. Although parentified, you were a child. The emotional labor you took on was never your responsibility, but you took it on anyway and that speaks volumes about your character. I know how thankful you are for your mother's insistence on allowing you to shape your identity. That is a blessing and a privilege not all children receive. Had it not been for that, who would you be? Even further, where would you be now that she's gone?

One day, you will have to learn to live without her and it will be hard. You won't want to do it. But you must and you will. You will live well not just without her but because of her. It's really the only thing you've ever truly been afraid of—life without her. But here it is. And look at you doing it! She knew you would need her, and she knew she wouldn't always be here so, she gave you everything you'd need before she left. Use it. Remember it. Make the most of it. Triple-double-quadruple her investment.

75

There is a time for the shadows but, at some point, you know you're meant to shine. You know who you are. So, this world's projections, lies, and manipulation fail at every turn.

Do you remember when you used to sit and record yourself playing for hours? Those were good times. You used to get so lost in the music that, when you went back and listened to the tapes (yes, tapes, girl; we're grown-grown now, lol), you wouldn't even remember doing what you heard yourself doing. You'd be like, "Wait, is that me?!" Yes, girl! That was YOU! That is still you. That will always be you.

Now, listen to me. This is important. I need you to know this and accept it as the truth that it is. You are not confused nor crazy. What you will experience with that man is not love. God has shown you love, and you know it by the sound. You know it by the way it falls on you like a sweet, heavenly fragrance. You'll know it. You always knew it.

Remember. There are men who will protect you. There are men who will provide for you. There are men who will speak life into and over you. There are men who will defend your name in your absence.

There are men who create and maintain safe spaces for you. These are the godly men in your life.

Trust those men. Love those men fiercely. Honor and revere these men. Theirs is the legacy you carry forward.

You are a blessed child. Your mom wasn't exaggerating or just being biased when she said that. (*Whispers* She wasn't lying when she told you that you weren't fat, too.) You are blessed. You'll see. Just keep living, like the elders used to say.

I'm telling you this, so you won't have to wonder. I've been where you're going, and it IS well.

It won't be funny, but you'll learn to laugh at the attempts of small men. They'll try and they will fail. Miserably. Comically. So, I take that back. Maybe it is a little bit funny to watch them make such fools of themselves.

Your joy is resistance, and your rage is justified and fair. You are graced to be proof that there is joy in the face of adversity. You are purposed to be proof that there is abundant life outside of self-sacrifice and abandonment. The very ones that will act like they don't see you will be the most inspired by you. Know that they see you and their validation is not integral to your existence. You are illuminating the path for someone who needs your light. So, shine. Shine without shame or guilt.

Somewhere along the way, I got so used to my needs being met with resistance and/or ignorance that I just stopped asking. I'm finding now that I may have just been asking/expecting my needs to be met by the wrong people.

Some people hold the title but, when you're a "strong woman," you have to surround yourself with people who can hold the weight.

In other words, everyone doesn't have the capacity to hold you. They may even genuinely want to, but some people just don't know how to.

Sometimes the last thing you need is another reminder of how strong you are. Sometimes it's just nice to not have to be. This may feel irrelevant to you now but, trust me, you'll need to know this later. Everybody that holds a "title" in your life won't be able to carry the weight of the anointing on your life. Some will even resent you for it because it's not them. Shake the dust. Hear me when I say it: Shake. The. Dust!

There are complete strangers who will like, love, and support everything you do. There are people you don't even know that will praise your name in rooms you may never step foot in. Your reputation will precede you. You will walk into rooms full of perceived strangers and receive the warmest reception because God goes before you.

Some people don't want what you give freely. They just want to be able to say they took something from you.

So, these people will do things like:

• Stalk your social media. (I know you have no idea what that is now, but trust me, you'll LOVE it later.)
• Constantly bring you up to others who are closer to you to (re)gain access and glean insights from them.
• Send others to do their dirty work because they're too cowardly to do it themselves.
• Allow unfounded rumors to stand without

challenge.

• Feign concern for you.

You will come to understand that most apologies tend to be more about absolving someone (offender) rather than repairing someone (offended/harmed).

Said another way, people often apologize to absolve themselves, not repair the person/people they hurt.

People will try their best to figure you out and be mad because they can't. That's not your problem.

People will make covert attempts to sabotage and undermine your success; they will also get mad when they fail. That's not your problem.

People will be mad because you're still smiling and laughing. That's not your problem.

People will create all kinds of narratives around you to make themselves feel better about how they (mis)treated you. That's not your problem.

People will sit on their hands until it's time to reach for the handout they feel entitled to. That's not your problem.

People will think they know you. They don't. And that's what? Not your problem!

(I hope you're noticing a pattern here.)

People just will. And that's not your problem. I have already told you what you're here for. Your purpose is made clear. All you have to do is stay focused, keep your heart pure, and your hands clean. Thank God for your purposeful life and keep living.

Don't let bitterness and resentment take root in your heart. It has no place there. Uproot the whole tree if you have to. Shake the dust and reestablish your roots in fertile ground. Some people will spend their whole lifetime pretending to be happy with their choices to avoid accountability. Let them.

These same people will remain committed to misunderstanding you because, to validate your feelings, they'd have to validate their own feelings that they refuse to acknowledge. It would be unwise to expect people who can't validate themselves to validate you. Move on. Time will tell the story better than you ever could anyway.

I know you remember Uncle Ed always speaking life into you. Never forget what he said. He was right and he loved you enough to make sure you knew from the start.

Laughter is medicine. So, surround yourself with people who are actually funny and not just funny-acting. Cultivate joy. Stay with the things, people, and places that inspire inside jokes, spark meaningful conversations, and allow levity to flow like water and ease to float like the aroma of your favorite food in the air.

Keep listening to that still, small voice, for it knows the way. Let it be your guide.

Replace trauma with triumph and exchange the pain for power. To God be the glory!

Remember those short story books you used to make with your cousin? Those are bestsellers now.

Remember those songs you used to make up? The ones you used to go upstairs and play while you waited for your mom after church? You get compensated well for those now.

Remember the answered prayers you've already lived.

These are the full circle moments you live for now. And there are plenty more where those came from. You already know this to be true. God has already shown you. Don't be surprised when you start to see what God said. Remember that God is working even when you're not.

You know who you are.

You are a blessed child. All you have to do now is walk it out. One foot in front of the other. One day at a time.

Right here.

Right now. With me. You are safe. You're alive and all is well.

It is well!

Love,
Charleeta (Me)

Multifaceted Black Girl

By Eternity Sledge

Dear Black Woman,

Between feeling surrounded instead of supported, dropping dead weight - aka people who never had any business in my vicinity, and transferring schools, I was going through a lot of changes at all times. I feel like I've lived more lives in the past 20+ years than some people ever experience. I was built for this type of life because I am Multifaceted, THEE Multifaceted Black Guide to be more precise.

This chapter will take you through my journey towards becoming a Multifaceted Black Guide and how it has affected me. WARNING: Shit gets real!

During my younger years, I pushed an ACE (Adverse Childhood Experience) to the back of my memory and tried to forget it ever happened. No one talks about what happens behind closed doors in many Black families, even less than they talk about how it affects them later. I too was a victim of playing "house" with my cousin, but I always felt like I was lucky because he didn't go all the way and so many others experienced that side. On the other hand, I always felt a little weird because it happened in my childhood bedroom, which I continued to stay in up until I left for college.

When you're young and innocent, you don't understand some of the things that occur to you and why they are wrong. You just see angry adults or people come around a little less, or even worse, get blamed for what went down because you "knew it was wrong, but did it anyway" … but did I? That was a memory I pushed away by pouring my energy into school and extracurricular activities.

Throughout those early years, I was extremely outgoing. Not only did I participate in band, cheerleading, plays, Math Bowls, and Student Council, but I was also attending a Performing Arts school during the summer, where I learned acting, modeling, and various forms of dance. Having my hand in so many buckets didn't bother me at all.

It felt great to hear the extensive list of accomplishments my teachers would read off at the award ceremonies. There would be so many that even the parents looked like they were over it, not mine though! My family would be right there taking pictures for Facebook with the biggest smiles on their faces because they knew I was special and that I could handle any obstacles put in front of me.

What they didn't know was that my biggest obstacle hadn't come yet.

In 6th - 8th grade, I started to learn about boys. My older cousin even taught me the 7 Bs: Books Before Boys Because Boys Bring Babies. I wasn't sure about how the boys brought the babies, but I knew they weren't going to bring one to me. I would keep up with what I saw some of the other girls doing, like texting boys on Kik and certain things they would say, but I would always get in trouble for it.

I even remember having a rule that I couldn't talk to boys, so instead of learning how to establish boundaries and about the playbook boys have, I was left ignorant to find out on my own. By the time I got to 8th grade, I still hadn't kissed a boy, but somehow, I stayed in trouble for talking to them.

At that point, I called myself getting a little boyfriend and hiding it from my parents until one day in math class, I got in trouble. For some odd reason, I decided to write Fuck You with a heart around it on that boy's arm. He asked to go to the bathroom, and the teacher saw his arm. She asked who did it, and he said he did it himself.

My teacher was not convinced. She came up to the people he was sitting next to and asked all of us who did it. I turned to her and thought about the number 1 rule in my house: don't lie because it will make your punishment worse. I told her that I did it, but he said I could - like that made it any better.

She told me she would tell my Homeroom teacher and let him decide what to do about it. He decided I deserved a detention and for him to call my parents. This meant I was going to lose my Valedictorian spot at graduation. It also meant I was going to be in big trouble when I got home. Eventually, my tears and the principal were able to convince my teacher not to write the detention, but to just call home. Little did I know at the time, calling my parents was worse.

I didn't get in much trouble for writing on his arm. The issue my parents had was the fact that I had a boyfriend. My two 8th-grade trips were taken from me, in addition to my phone and the warmth my parents usually gave me. It felt cold and isolating being surrounded but not feeling supported. That was the first time I began to have symptoms of depression.

However, I didn't have the vocabulary or knowledge to recognize what was occurring. Since this incident was a few months before my school trips, my teachers and band directors were speaking up on my behalf. They believed that I was a good kid who deserved to attend the two trips, even with the mistake I had made. Somehow, they convinced her, so I was still able to go on that trip, yet there was something that had changed in me, something was different.

I've always heard that high school was the good years, the glory days and such, but for me it was a long, drawn-out sentence that I had to serve because I was growing up. The high school that was blessed with my presence made the cut for one reason; it had the least amount of stairs. I did not want to deal with stairs—every day, so I chose a school that only had 3 steps, which could be avoided with a ramp.

My freshman year was rough. I had lost my great-grandmother, who helped me learn how to bake, taught me how to play card games, and would love to have sleepovers with me. This was the first time I was ever near the front row for a funeral. That year was also when I got put on the worst punishment I had experienced thus far.

My parents went out of town and my cousin was supposed to come check on me as my "babysitter" even though I was at least 14-15 years old. I had a new boyfriend at the time, who convinced me to let him come over to the house. And before you start thinking something crazy, I was a virgin, and all we did was watch TV and cuddle until it was time for him to go.

My dad found out because me and the boy fell asleep on FaceTime. He came in my room and asked me who I was on the phone with. Half asleep, I tell him "my boyfriend," which in hindsight was not the right answer, but was the truth. As a good parent would, he checked my phone and read the messages about the boy coming to the house. Everything went downhill from there.

Of course, I got a whooping and my phone taken, but I wasn't expecting to have to author a paper on self-love, read a book about Derek Jeter, and not go back in my room unless it was to get a change of clothes. No phone, no radio, no TV. Nothing but a book, a couch, a paper, and me. I would get random tasks around the house, like painting walls.

The most vivid memory I have is the black circular mirror that was hung in the living room. I sprayed it with glass cleaner and looked at myself when I wiped it off. It felt like a scene in the movies when everything slows down and you just know something weird is about to happen. As I looked at myself, I heard a voice in my head say, "Drink it. Drink the Windex. No one will miss you." I hesitated for a while and eventually shook the thought away, but by then I knew something was wrong. I needed help.

I told my parents that I thought I may have been depressed. They told me to "go find a therapist" and "it's probably just a phase." I felt neglected, unsupported, and alone. Present day, I believe they didn't understand depression at the time. They may have also thought that was my way of trying to get

91

out of my punishment because we wouldn't get told how long we were in trouble for. We'd just come home one day and get invited to watch a movie or to get food and that would be the end of the punishment.

Sophomore through senior year, the outgoing and joyful Eternity didn't grace the halls of the high school. The version of me that showed up was mean, sad, and a loner. I operated like a chameleon, blending in with whichever group I was around at the time. Throughout this transformation, one thing that didn't change was pouring myself into everything I could.

Despite no longer valuing my life, I was a member of the Varsity Cheerleading team, Marching & Concert Band, Latin Club, AP & Honors Classes, and more. I had overheard my mother once say, "An empty mind is the devil's playground," so I kept myself busy up until I left for college.

Finally, it was time for college. I was so excited for the opportunity to be independent. Day 1, I met one of my best friends to this day, who had lived across the hall from me. I also had to share a room for the first time, outside of sleepovers with my friends. My roommate barely acknowledged my existence but made sure I knew she was there each night.

After walking pass me on the streets and not speaking, a light brighter than the sun would shine out of her lamp so she could flip the loudest pages in a book almost every single night. This was irritating, but something I could deal with. What I did not like was how messy her side of the room was. There were wrappers, utensils, papers, and other random things splayed across the floor. To the point I had to tell her if I see a bug, I am going to throw everything in the dorm away.

Later, I met someone who had basically become my sister because of the way we clicked and bonded so well. Let's call her Layla. Layla and I would do everything together, from grocery shopping to ice cream dates to Sunday dinners. One day, the girl from across the hall, Layla, and one other girl were trying to reach me. They had been calling and texting, but I wasn't responding.

I was in my room under my bed lying on a huge bean bag chair in the fetal position crying most of that day. Life had become so overwhelming between being an RA, working at a grocery store, being on Executive Boards, and studying biomedical engineering. I had been to therapy that summer, but the school was in a different state, so my therapist couldn't see me anymore.

Eventually, the girls stopped trying to call and just came to my apartment. They opened my door and saw me on the floor crying. That was a very vulnerable moment for me that I don't think they realized I truly needed at the time. After that situation, I decided to withdraw from the university on mental leave because I wanted to come back with a strong mind and the tools in place to handle those times.

The plan was for me to stay in Layla's spare room while I found an apartment. That plan changed soon after because her family came to pick her up, I took over her lease, and I never heard from her again. This was one of the worst heartbreaks of my life. She was more than a friend to me. It was like I lost my other half, so I did like most girls do when their hearts get broken, I took care of myself and started my transformational journey towards leveling up.

I began to practice gratitude, say affirmations daily, and I produced a plan called Becoming That Girl. I outlined how I wanted all aspects of my life to look, and I got to work. These aspects ranged from how I wanted to make money to wanting to communicate efficiently and effectively to something as simple as drinking water.

At the time, I was working three part-time jobs and doing an internship, but this didn't feel like alignment with "Becoming That Girl." One day, I burst out in tears at the register during a cashier shift. I was writing down on the back of a receipt all the things I wish I had and the things I appreciated having. One of the things was not to have to be on my feet all day. A few weeks later, I traded in those three jobs for one job as a Marketing Coordinator. I was doing great until I got into a car accident and totaled my car.

All that healing and challenging work just to be catching an Uber to work and sitting with an idle mind for the devil to play in almost left me devastated, but that's when I got accepted into my HBCU. I was excited for a change of scenery, meeting new people, and a new major, Elected

Studies, which meant I could take whatever classes I wanted. I didn't last long in the dorm room because I wasn't used to those conditions, so I got an apartment off campus. This was when I stepped into the second-best version of myself.

I had begun branding myself as a Multifaceted Black Girl on stage for my poetry performances and on my clothing brand. So many people tried to put me in a box by telling me "You need to choose a niche," "you're too young to start a business," or "you do everything, don't you?" I was a poet who sold custom T-shirts, started a subscription box, worked as a Virtual Assistant, while getting a degree as a full-time student, leading on multiple Executive Boards, interning at various companies, and joining a sorority. So yes, I do everything.

While visiting back home during a long weekend, I heard my mother shriek out a familiar, but heartbreaking scream. We found out my cousin's life was taken. Nothing could have prepared me for the rollercoaster of emotions I felt over the next few weeks. Back and forth trips home, funerals, candle-lighting ceremonies, classes, work, and a dog were taking everything out of me.

The only way I could think to turn my pain into positivity was to start a nonprofit youth organization that would keep my cousin's legacy alive. Something that all of my family members could use their passions and talents to contribute to. Along with Mirkat Impact Foundation being born, my desire to be with my family increased.

After graduating from undergraduate, I had a 2-bedroom, 2.5-bathroom rental townhouse, a dog, a new car, and an insurance job in my college's town that would allow me to live an amazingly comfortable life. Somehow, I found myself applying for an online Master's Program, which turned into being accepted for the 9-month in-person program in my home state.

I had a huge choice to make between my comfortable, COVID-proof job or going to get a degree that costs the amount of my salary and moving home with no job. Ultimately, I chose to be a broke college student again because I was a hopeful Multifaceted Black Girl. Little did I know that broke was about to turn into broken, again.

Self-care has always been a difficult battle for me because the goalpost never stopped. My goals kept growing, changing, and elevating to the point where I didn't feel I deserved to celebrate myself. I started to feel like the major milestones I accomplished were the standard rather than something special. One of the even harder battles for me, though, was grief. Losing friends, family, and worst of all, losing my maternal grandmother.

My grandmother was a wise, sharp, beautiful soul who was devoted to God and her children. I spent some time taking care of her because her lungs weren't the best. We talked and I asked questions because it was my first time being truly one-on-one with her. I continued to visit her randomly, but my favorite visit was on her last birthday.

She didn't know I was coming, and she was so surprised and happy to see me. I pulled out my notebook with my questions and asked her if she could do anything right now, what she would do. She told me she would "get better and spread the word of God." Her words gave me goosebumps and began my journey to deepening my relationship with God and becoming her disciple.

One month before I started my master's program, my grandmother passed away. She and her youngest grandson were reconnected. The numbers 11:11 continuously popped up for me afterward. I assumed that was her way of letting me know she was still with me and guiding me in the right direction. She is where I developed my values that my identity is built on: family, freedom, and faith. She instilled the value of family supporting, loving, and caring for each other, no matter what, especially siblings.

My grandmother left people alone who didn't align with her values. She freed herself from them, including her husband, and freed herself from society's opinions. Every morning my grandmother would be on the prayer call while she was sick. We would watch the gospel network, and she would tell me stories about her faith in God. She was a beautiful representation of walking by faith in my life.

Becoming her disciple meant that I was no longer a Multifaceted Black Girl. I was now a catalyst of transformation, a community builder, and most importantly, a Multifaceted Black Guide supporting others on their journeys as she did for me.

Let my journey be a reminder that life is all about transformation, which starts with your mindset. Transformation doesn't happen overnight. You may be in a place where you feel lost, isolated, or surrounded by chaos. Don't let your fear take over your thoughts. Remember Faith over fear because the dark times end and the light will come. When it does come don't dim it, put it in a box, or lose it because of the actions of someone else.

Black Woman, love you the way you desire everyone else to love you and you will attract your most delusional reality because Black Women are the blueprint, and we set the tone!

Love,
Multifaceted Black Girl Guide
aka Eternity Sledge

Purpose
and
Partnership

By Dr. Kim Thomas Manning

Dear Black Woman,

Do you remember the cute, little girl that you were?
What about the sometimes difficult teenager you
were? I know you remember the young lady you
were, the one who knew everything about
everything. Reach back, look at the little girl, the
teenager, and the young lady you were in her eyes,
and share some WOW (Words of Wisdom) with her.
The little girl within needs the WOW that can only
come from the mature you, Black Woman.

Wisdom comes from many places: the hard places,
the lonely places, the scared places, the how-I-made
it over places, the triumphant places.

Dear Black Woman, as a little girl, you may have
been taught to expect the fairytale life of graduating
from high school, going to college, meeting your
college sweetheart, marrying him, starting a family,
buying a house, and living the all-American dream.
Others of you may have experienced so much
trauma that a fairytale life was not in the cards for
you, and you expected a hard life because that's just
the way it is. That's life. Neither experience is right
or wrong, each experience is just so. The story I

share is somewhere in between. It is a story of love, joy, difficulty, and loneliness mixed with triumphant and *"Thank-you Jesus"* moments.

Dear Black Woman, I thought I had done all the right things, all the things that were expected of me. I earned excellent grades throughout my secondary school years. My place as class valedictorian was secure. I earned academic scholarships for college. I attended one of two historically Black universities (known as HBCUs) in my home state. Those were the only options. It did not matter that I received letters of interest from colleges and universities all over the country. Grambling State University was it. That was one of the two HBCUs. My mother and my aunt had gone there; I would matriculate there as well. After-all, it was a three-hour drive away from home, and it set me apart from most of my family members who attended Southern University. Little Black girl, curious Black teenager, choices matter. Options matter. Your voice matters. If you see options for your life's journey, tell someone what those options are. Tell someone what you would like to do for yourself, even if it is not the options that were laid out and predestined for you.

I met my future husband during my second semester at GSU. I was swept off of my feet by the attention, the compliments, the idea of having a boyfriend. There were many warning signs that he was not the one, but I ignored them. I didn't trust the young lady I was and the young lady I was becoming. How did she really know what a healthy romantic relationship looked like, anyway? She didn't.

He was not a practicing Christian. He was not excelling academically. We had many different values, and our families of origin were vastly different. Dear little Black girl, dear college student who wants to fit in, you do not have to fit in. We are fearfully and wonderfully made just as our Heavenly Father created us to be. Dear little Black girl who may not have had a father/daughter relationship in which you learned how males should treat you, there is no need to look for love in all the wrong places. Let love find you. Take care of your spiritual self, your psychological self, your financial self. Learn all that you can learn. Earn that post-secondary certificate. Earn that degree or degrees. Do so in preparation to take care of yourself.

104

Those are two snippets from my life, but neither is the focus I have chosen for this anthology.

For those of you asking what happened with my college sweetheart, of course I married him. That's what you were supposed to do. Go to college. Find the person who would become your spouse. Get married in a big, Southern, church wedding. And live happily ever after. The happy-ever-after did not happen, but that's a story for a different anthology.

Almost three years into the anticipated happily-ever-after, my then-husband shared that he wanted a child. I had a different idea. I wanted to go to graduate school. Why not? The company I worked for would pay for everything, even books. We decided (I'll use that word loosely) to do both. I do not recall the exact date I started my MBA program, but we started trying to get pregnant around the same time, and it wasn't long before I was taking classes with a big pregnant belly that required a different seating arrangement during my last quarter of the program.

The pregnancy was pretty uneventful. I went to work. I went to class at night. I did jazzercise at the local community center. I went to every prenatal doctor's visit. I took my prenatal vitamins as I was instructed. I didn't smoke. I didn't drink. I should have had a perfect labor and delivery and perfect postpartum recovery. Right? Wrong! December 5, 1992, was a day that would change my life forever!

My mother arrived two weeks early for the birth of her first grandchild. She even flew to get there. She did not like to fly, but that was an event worthy of taking a flight. She accompanied me to my last visit before my due date. The doctor said the baby was a little small (should have been a red flag because neither parent was small), but everything was moving as expected.

The evening before my due date, we had planned to have pizza for dinner. What else do you eat for dinner when you are nine months pregnant with your first child, and you and your husband are both still in your twenties? Pizza, of course.

My then-husband had gone to work, and he was expected to be home soon. In the meantime, I started having an uncomfortable feeling, but I would not classify the feeling as pain. I mentioned it to my mother, who insisted I call my doctor. I didn't want to, but I complied. My doctor was not on call, but the on-call doctor told me to go to the hospital to "check everything out" since my due date was the next day.

I complained for the entire 20-30 minutes it took to drive from Smyrna, GA to Crawford Long Hospital in Atlanta, GA. I just knew that I was not in labor. This is not how labor was described during the birthing classes. I knew that the doctor would send us home because I wasn't in labor. I am sure that the doctor was going to be annoyed because we wasted her time with this false alarm. Boy, was I wrong!

Dear young Black woman, you do not know everything. There are elders who have been where you have yet to go. They have amassed an arsenal of experiences that you do not have. I am grateful that I listened to my mother that evening.

The drama leading to the trauma had begun. The attending doctor examined me and could not find the baby's heartbeat. First call to my physician's office. Try to get the heartbeat vaginally. Nothing. My water had not broken. Second call to my

107

physician's office. The attending physician received specific orders: Break her water. Done. Uh-oh. Meconium aspiration. My unborn baby had a bowel movement in utero. This could get real bad real fast. I heard, "Prep for emergency c-section."

After the fact, you can always identify something funny that happened in the midst of a traumatic event. The nurse asked my then-husband to change into a set of disposable scrubs for the operating room. I implored, "Ma'am, he can't wear that." The nurse responded, "It's one size fits all." My then-husband was a big man. Sure enough, he put one leg into the disposable scrub, and rip. The nurse went to find real scrubs! Well, I told her so.

Off to the operating room we go. I was watching a movie, except I wasn't. This was my life happening in living color. Kabria was delivered. There was no time to waste. She was in an incubator. They whisked her to the Neonatal Intensive Care Unit (NICU). I didn't know it at the time, but I was grieving. I had carried another human being in my body for nine months, and now that human was no longer inside of me. I did not have the words back then, but grief is it - a traumatic loss. Dear Black

108

Woman, claim and name whatever you are feeling. If we do not name it, we cannot heal it.

I don't really remember much after Kabria was whisked away. My next memory is in my hospital room. My mom is there. The curtains are drawn; it's drab inside. I think there were congratulatory balloons and flowers. I just don't remember. I do, however, remember the on-call doctor who delivered Kabria. She came into the room with a barrage of questions: Do you smoke? Do you do recreational drugs? Have you been sick? What kind of insurance do you have? Of all the questions, the one about my insurance coverage irked me the most. In my mind, my doctor should be concerned about my well-being and the well-being of the human she helped usher into this world. She may have been, but her words and actions did not say she empathized with me at all. Dear Black Woman, you deserve expert medical care, whether you have top-notch medical insurance or not. I was covered. I had good insurance, but still, the question was asked shortly after the trauma I had just experienced and continued to process. Dear Black Woman, you are allowed to ask questions of your health care providers. You are your own best advocate. If something isn't right, or if something doesn't feel right in your interactions with healthcare providers, speak up. Say something. Document and report the wrongs. Little Black Girl, you may not have been able to advocate for yourself back then, but now that you are a strong, confident Black Woman, advocate for yourself, for your family, for your community, and for the greater good. You have the power.

I had the immense pleasure of having a friend who is still the most positive person I know. When she came to visit me, her bubbly personality lit up the room. She'd brought flowers or balloons (I can't remember which.) She threw open the blinds exclaiming that we should be rejoicing that our situation was not worse than it was. My mother sat there silently. When my friend left, my mother moaned, shook her head, and said my friend didn't know how serious the situation was. My friend did know, but she was an optimistic person. She believed in God's power to change circumstances, and she wanted me to feel better. Kim, the little girl, needed that sense of optimism. Dear little Kim, it is

okay to be hopeful. It is okay to be positive.
Circumstances do not define you.

Now, I am engaged in a different kind of grief. I was
grieving the feeling of carrying another human being
in my womb. I was grieving the perfect newborn I
thought I'd have. Now, I was grieving the
relationship I wish I'd had with my mother. I have
now accepted that my mother did the best she could
with what she had, but she did not have the
emotional bandwidth to support me.

I would go on to experience other major life events
that I may have handled differently if I had had
empathy and compassion from my mother. If I could
go back to the little girl I was, I would hug her,
smother her with kisses, and let her know she was
enough. Enough of everything. If I could go back to
the twenty-six year old me that was a new mom in a
traumatic situation, I would say, "I am so sorry that
you are going through this, but I am with you. I will
not let you travel this road alone. We will get
through this. Everything will be alright."

Understanding my mother's inability to offer
emotional support has had a lingering effect on me

to this very day. Dear Black Woman, put your guard down. You don't have to be the strong Black woman all the time. Someone needs your tenderness, your compassion, your empathy. Saying, "This is just the way I am," is unacceptable. Everyone can change. Embrace the emotional side of you. Strive for an elevated level of emotional intelligence. The little girl you were needed it; now, you can give it to someone else.

The nightmare wasn't over. I don't know what my initial reaction was when I saw Kabria in the NICU. There were tubes everywhere! She was not, by far, the sickest baby in the NICU, but she was my baby. There was nothing I could do at that moment to make things better. I vowed right there that I would always fight for her.

I spent three days in the hospital after my c-section. When I was discharged, I told Kabria I would be back to see her the next day. The next day arrived. My father and my grandmother had made the trip to Atlanta, and they wanted to see Kabria. I started getting dressed. Remember, I had just had a c-section. A momma, a grandmother, and a daughter/granddaughter who had just had a c-section a few days earlier—can you imagine that combination.

I needed to heal. I didn't need to get out in the cold. My pores needed to close (according to the two older women). It was winter in Atlanta, but I prepared to see my baby. My parents and grandmother were concerned because I had only had surgery three days prior, but my husband sensed what I was feeling, and he defied everyone else and said he was taking me to see our daughter. Dear Black Woman, sometimes love requires that you defy what you know intellectually to be common sense. Love may require putting yourself at risk for the ones you love. I was not healed from the c-section, but I had made a promise to Kabria. Promises made should be promises kept. Dear little Kim, you deserve to expect that when someone makes a promise to you, the promise will be kept.

Writing and reliving this experience has been painful! There are few people who have heard this much of my story. Believe me, there's more. But, through the pain, I know that Little Kim and Dr. Kim are both healing in ways that they did not have the opportunity to heal before.

113

At the time of this writing, Kabria is 32 years old. She has profound disabilities. Physically, she is relatively healthy. She loves her family; she has an infectious smile; and she loves going to church. She doesn't realize it, but her life is a light, an example of God's unconditional love.

With Love,
Kim

Love
In the
Flesh

By Loren Simon

We're All New to This Thing

Dear Lo,

In recent weeks, your mother found a photo of you when you were six. Do you remember that green and blue swimsuit that you loved? It was a picture of you having a fun summer day in the yard, playing in the sprinklers as most kids coming up in the early 2000's did. You seemed so full of joy, but I recall your inner voice at that time. It would be negligent to not provide you with the space to say the words that you undoubtedly felt, and I will provide that space for you. Albeit, the teenage and early twenties year old Loren has not been the kindest to you, I want you to know that in your late twenties, Loren, you fight every day to protect and honor yourself.

This is my love letter to you. To show you my devotion and thankfulness for who you were then and who you are now.

To be you has never been easy. You were a whimsical child who saw vibrancy everywhere. You spoke with wisdom beyond your years-not comprehending how you could know so much

116

without having lived enough. You read books with a passion and spoke with kindness at each possible turn. You could sense and feel the emotions of others, see angels in the sky, become one with music, and LOVE. Girl you were love in the flesh! But over the years you were told to be quiet. To shrink yourself literally and figuratively because you were bigger than all the other little girls. To not express what you perceived to be right and wrong, for fear that you would answer incorrectly. To take on a level of maturity that robbed you of your chance to truly be a child. You put on the coat of thousands of Black girls everywhere. The coat of forced "black" womanhood. You held higher responsibility and expectation than your brother. You were appointed as the golden child. The smart one. The one who had to have her plan ready from the very beginning. You had to stop dreaming around the age of 8 and you did for a while. Around that time is when you became silent. It is when you began your sentence of centering the approval of others and living life outside of your being. I lost you. I needed you. But here I am to bring you out of hiding. If you don't mind, let me catch you up on all that has happened.

117

You remember your formative years rather well, so I'll start from where I came in contact with you again. It was August of 2016 at age 18 that you entered undergrad at the best historically Black institution this side of the Mississippi, The GREAT Bethune-Cookman University! You earned yourself a vocal and merit scholarship that year, fulfilling a path your grandmother was too scared to take, and your mother didn't complete. Holding the task of following through exceptionally, you committed yourself to four years. There was no room for any other option but excelling. So, you struggled when you had to. You braved a face when you had to. You pushed through heartbreak and betrayal when you had to because walking the road your forebears couldn't meant the world to you. Anxiety stayed on your tail, but you always pushed. You did it scared. You sang in front of audiences, scared. You performed at NATS, scared. Voice shaking and heartbeat racing. You never let that stop you. You had a voice professor who believed in you but more than that, she loved you. Her care helped you to confront fear and soar in your own way. She saw your tears and helped you become strong. She pushed you. You gave her all that you had. She gave you the acceptance that others could not. Dr. Hundley rooted for you. He became your adopted uncle. Dr. Grace spoke to your intelligence, never undermining the way you interpreted the art form of music. She became family as well. Little do they know, they all protected that little girl on the inside of you. They knew you were a college student then, but they saw past that current iteration of you. They saw the little girl who needed softness, guidance, and strength. Even with their investments in you, that did not shield you from the hurt that was deep inside or the hurt that you would run into during your years there. Senior year, it all came crashing down. After fighting to be understood and trying your best to be tolerable, you found yourself isolated. The friends you thought you had, began to drift. The "here today, gone tomorrow" attention/affections of a couple of boys proved to make nothing more than a bowl of nothing. You became numb and anxious all the time. You were on medication for a year due to it. Your mother was worried sick. That burden took you to some very dark places. Deep inside, we felt that there was little to no hope of being loved anymore. Not by friends, not by lovers, not by anyone. The inner voice that sculpted you drove us into deep depression. The days got harder and harder to live. Reciprocation from those you gave too, no longer existed. Instead, blame was our portion. Yet, in the midst of the darkness, that is when you showed up. After years of repression, you turned your face to me.

Now that you know what has happened to you, let me tell you the story of how we made it out. I had to face you. In the years of floating in lukewarm vats of emptiness, I woke up one day and decided to practice the art of Sankofa. To go back and get what was left behind. You see, we had always been taught to abandon ourselves, Loren. That is all we knew! But I could see your face, scared with the ever-present fear that nobody was coming to stand up for you. It was like seeing you locked up in the corner of your room within a house that had no oil lamp or fireplace. Rocking yourself with arms wrapped tight around your body just aching to feel some form of love. Any small gesture of care. Just a little relief from the constant rejection that played on a loop in your head. You were there. You became my mission and reason for becoming well. Through therapy, self-reflection, trial and error, I took the keys and opened the almost rusted front door.

The foyer of our mind filled with the kind of nothingness that stilled the air in a room. Calling out for you did no good because you did not seek to pull the load this time. Instead, I looked up the staircase of memories and let my feet feel each landing board. Every scene played out like it was brand new. A feeling akin to daggers would pierce me, but I had to get to you. So, I kept climbing those stairs. I cried on the stairs. I sat down on the stairs. I cursed the stairs for being what they were. But I kept climbing. Once I made it to the top, the hallway was the next quest. With its walls nearly bare, except for the faded images of experiences, the hall was something like a looking glass. Every memory amplified but ghostly. Relics of old dreams juxtaposed to the realities, a rather haunting pastoral scene spread across multiple frames. Arriving at the door, I stopped and listened. I wanted to hear a cry…maybe a whimper. Something that could realize the distress I felt in my soul. But you were silent. Opening the door, I saw you sitting and holding yourself in a cradle fashion. Eyes full of tears that quietly rolled down your

121

cheeks. It took you a moment to realize I was there but once you noticed that it was me in the doorway, you looked up. No words were exchanged immediately. All I knew was that someone I loved was hurt and I had to comfort them. Looking into your eyes, I assured you that I would get your voice back. Feelings of protection for you washed over me as did the embrace that I gave you. The exchange told me that you needed to be reparented. Specifically, you needed to be re-mothered.

Re-mothering is acknowledging that your upbringing could have resulted in loose ends, holes in the story, and abandonment. Of course, the degree of which that affects you is personal and is not to be taken lightly at any time. Our mother is a loving woman who would do and still does anything that she can for her babies. She has made you and your siblings her joy. The very thrill of her life comes from seeing her children with large smiles. As a child, you did not have the luxury of prolonged happiness. Your mother worked ridiculously hard and gave you what she had left over from that day. She did her best to shower you with homework help, hugs, kisses, and laughs because she knew what it was like to have a parent who controlled her expression. Your mother is many wonderful things, but she was not a woman of confidence. You believed your mother to be beautiful in heart, mind, and soul. You wanted to be just like her. Color your hair like her. Have spunk and originality like her. Laugh like her. Love like her. The woman you saw was your textbook definition of a woman until you learned of her weaknesses. Those weaknesses begat places of unsureness in you. The more others played into her weaknesses, the more you mirrored her lived experience. So I had to become your mother.

The first element in the plan was coming clean that I was not perfect, nor would I be on this new journey. We had to be on the same page for it to work. I let you in on all of the secret fears, the regrets, and the emotions that were hidden. You deserved to know why I had to drown out your begs of inclusion. In some ways, I was ashamed of having to lean into you out of fear that I would not be considered as a woman worth listening to. What I failed to realize was that the battle was between you and what everyone else wanted you to be. As your mother, I now provide you with space to communicate with me without any pretense. No formal modes. No expectancy in a delivery. The raw truth, as you knew it to be, is all that I need. I can tell that you appreciate this autonomy by your "when." You speak when you feel it's necessary. It is often quick and simple. Mostly, single sentences. If you're not speaking verbally, you touch my heart with warmth if you like or love something. An internal smile that is angelic and soft.

The second element was urging you to feel. Feeling is what we used to do all of the time, but somewhere along the way, we lost that. It could have been when your grandparents made fun of you for being quick to cry. It could have been when your father did not show up to any of your chorus concerts in high school. It could have been when you witnessed your mother having a severe breakdown where she felt completely void of any love whatsoever. It could have been when you reasoned that your father never truly wanted children and thus never knew what to make out of you and your siblings. It could have been as a teenager when you felt as though no boys wanted you because you weren't like the other girls. You grew stone cold in a way. Getting you to feel once more meant letting you cry as often and about whatever you wanted. Sitting in it with you and reaffirming that you were safe to mourn, be overjoyed, or happy so much that you dance without any inhibitions was like watching you be reborn. For about a year, we worked on sitting in the feelings. Any time you had the urge to run away, I was right there to hold you. But, just as any good mother, I had to redirect you. After you could put words to what you felt, I had to help you frame it all. You were not overly sensitive. You were compassionate. Teaching you what compassion was by giving you it was like watching a child learn how to ride a bike for the first time. In any circumstance that provoked robust feelings in you, it was as if I could see you on your bike and yelling, "I'm doing it!" You sat in those emotions. There were times when your head began to swim but I was your lifeguard. Never would there ever be a time when you felt as though you were braving the world alone if I could help it.

Element three in the plan showed itself to be allowing you to experiment. This was hard for me and still is because of the chance of hurt that exists. Nevertheless, I did what you wanted to do. We tried that adult ballet class to defy the bogus belief that larger little girls (now women) were not the proper size for the art. Lo and behold, you did so well and felt free! The euphoria you felt in that moment resulted in confident leaps across the classroom floor. Small giggles present throughout the entire class. No care in the world that you were one of two Black women there. All you cared about was showing up in that moment as the chubby little girl that could move with the best of them. You tested the waters with new relationships, which was difficult due to the little you knew about how to arrive in relationships. But we trusted each other. I trusted you to let me know when a circumstance didn't feel right. You trusted me in guiding you either from it or alongside it.

What I did not know about you that I learned in experimenting was that your love has flexibility. You were fully present in being and voice when I began dating after a major heartbreak. You gave me the green light to have a form of trust with someone new who was more than you thought they would be. When the connection had to be broken due to me not feeling as though it was the right thing to do, you did not hide your sadness. The thought of having to let someone down or hurting them made tears fall in open confession to them. Instead of choking those feelings, you told me to let them be. The assuredness from the man that all was well calmed you. We woke up the next day a little unsure on whether we made the right decision, but you told me that we did. And guess what you did next? You kept on living. It was as though you fell off the bike, scraped up your knee, but got right back on it after the wound was cleaned and bandaged. That flexibility of knowing that your love had the resilience to love past transition and to where it didn't feel fatal…moved me beyond words.

It is true that in a perfect world or in another set up of life, I would not have had to re-mother you Loren. I could have grown into who I was to be in each phase of life with some sort of clarity and security. There would have been no need for backtracking and correcting many faults in the foundation of who you are. But let's say that it was that way. What good would it have brought me if I did not have this moment right now? Being your mother has been one of the most rewarding walks I have done in my life

127

so far. You have brought me joy once I realized that you are joy. Your peace gave me permission to accept peace for the gift that it is. Your enthusiasm for life produced a thirst for the richest of memories that I want to make. Your passion for living your truest life has become our life's purpose. Mothering you has taught me how to nurture seeds that have fallen on hard ground. The seeds themselves are fragile but have every code for their life inside of them. Their shell can only withstand so much before all is exposed and the only time they will grow to become fruit or flower is if somebody takes the initiative to see it through past its potential. Likewise, your shell had gotten cracked, parts of you were exposed to the elements, but here you are. Yet another beautiful crop. Are there times when I fail you as a mother? Yes. There are times when we do not see eye to eye. You want one thing, but I may know another. In moments such as these, you and I are now able to bring forth our dispositions and decide the path that would be favorable for you and me. I would like to suggest that this works due to the both of us pushing past the want and prioritizing the needs. Now we can love while being free of internal binds.

Now, re-parenting yourself requires an inexplicable level of transparency and commitment to who you are in the present but who you were in the past. There is no future "you" without those first two people. There is no reality where you as a child and you as an adult will exist separately. You are always one. That is why Sankofa is such a skillful gift. It contradicts the notion of not looking back because there is nothing to see. Instead, it says "look back but know what you are looking for." In the case of the parent wound, it means to look for what was missing. It does not mean to look at just the areas of lack but what may have caused the lack. If you can find those jars, then you can begin to test their capacities. You have to walk through the stages of victimhood from start to finish: 1) Being the victim, 2) Needing to be the victim, 3) Wanting to be the victim, 4) Letting go of being the victim, and 5) Choosing to be more than a victim. Why? You may ask. Because you are so much more than what has ever happened to you. You are more than what your parents could not see. You are more than what your mother could not foster in you. You are not just talents or skills. You are a being that exists in the intersection of the physical and the supernatural.

There is no conceivable way that those who were selected to usher you into this realm know exactly what you will need. That journey is for you. You may not want it to be, but that is the truth. So now, you get to be the parent that you desire. You have the chance to spend Friday nights stimulating your imagination. You have the space to be as free emotionally as you need. You get to return to living with your body and not outside of it via the pleasing of others or mindless chasing of societal success.

You may not "fix" every parent-rooted issue. There will be times that the memories play back at the loudest volume. You will presently want them to show up for eight year old you. I urge you to resist the inclination to push your inner child away when these feelings arise. Hold her tight! Reassure her of what her present life is like with you at the helm. Remember that she doesn't need another lesson on survival. She needs to learn how to land softly. The more you find solace and possibility in practicing Sankofa, the more grace you find for yourself and your mother. Every person has a capacity and maybe your mother met hers. That has nothing to do with how much capacity you can hold for yourself. It has nothing to do with all the ways you can find to present love to yourself.

Love. We as women speak about love so much that it has virtually become a dull subject that is full of imagination. That is, we speak about a love that we can only dream of because we are not certain that love can find us and hold us as we are. Who are we to demand a love that fulfills in that way? Who are we to offer that kind of love with no contract of reciprocity? The fear sets in soon after; shutting off any entry way for love to flow. There are times that I join the caravan and ride for a while as well. I would be lying if I claimed to always believe that such deep love that I imagine could exist for me. Learning you through the eyes of a mother has built up that confidence Loren. The more I get to know you, the more I want to know! The more I let you live in our right now, the more I can release the past hurts that forced you into isolation. Most importantly, the more I love you, the more I can see why love is possible for us. You keep me content in child-like splendors when the world is yelling for all of us to "grow up" for the machine. I smile at who I see in the morning because I have come to love you.

131

Compliments flow easy from my mouth when I create or have a delicious thought. There is no limit to how much I am willing to let love flow from us and back to us because you have declared that love is who you are. Loren, there are many years left ahead of us in this journey of life. Many years that God has laid ahead for us to do groundbreaking kingdom work. Many years that could be filled with joy and pain. As your mother, I am telling you now, we will be alright. As yourself...Loren, we will rise from love, in love, and to love. Thank you for meeting me here. Thank you for being ready to be all of you. In this lifetime and any that I'm not even sure of, I love you and I am grateful to be you.

Eternally Yours,
Loren.

Power of Words

By Mauryunna Brown

You Are Enough

Dear Little Maury

"This life is one of testing. Testing all patience. Testing all resilience." Shelly-Ann Gajadhar

In this life, we will encounter many things. Some we will deem as "good" and some we will deem as "bad." I want you to know, little me, that I am proud of you for making it through all moments. I am proud of you for never giving up and continuing to push forward no matter what trials appeared upon our path. In the moments of solitude that brought forth enlightenment and growth, you never wavered.

I am extremely proud of every version of you, of me, of us, that we have evolved to become. I want you to know you are enough. You always have been. From what seems like the beginning of this life, you encountered emotions of feeling as though you weren't enough. Your first memory being your mother's first suicide attempt at the tender age of two years old. Seeing her being wheeled away on a stretcher, and vividly remembering that moment, this was the first mark left upon your heart. You thought, maybe it was your fault.

Maybe… if you were a better child, a better person, cried less, did less, sat still, behaved as a "good girl" should, then maybe she wouldn't have decided to attempt to take her life. You allowed yourself to carry those emotions, those burdens, for as long as you can remember. I want you to know it is okay to lay them down. They are not yours to carry. It was never your fault. None of it was.

When Dad left, it had nothing to do with you. He made the decision to leave because he felt that was what was best for him. His leaving imprinted those feelings of being unlovable, unimportant, and tangible deep within the depths of your subconscious and soul. These feelings caused flawed inner beliefs rooted in abandonment. However, his actions have NEVER been a reflection of your worth, of our worth. It is okay to release those feelings of not belonging; of not being enough to be wanted, loved, or cared for. We have always been lovable. We have always been important. We do, we matter. You matter!

As we have journeyed, we have learned to do our best not to take things personally. Though, I know that is a tough thing to do, it is imperative so you may be at peace. So, we may be at peace. If we continue to carry the burdens of the past, we will only be weighed down. Ultimately, attracting those same experiences into our life because we haven't released what is no longer serving us.

It is okay to let it all go. You are enough. You deserve the love, the peace, the joy you desire. We will receive it, but only when we first decide to give it to ourselves. No one else has ever been the deciding factor in your worth, in our worth. You have always been worthy. You have always been enough.

As a child, and even in young adulthood, you dealt with so much comparison. Mom always comparing you, "Why can't you be like her?" "Why won't you dress this way." Relatives projecting onto you as though you simply being yourself is not acceptable. "Don't wear lip-gloss, your lips are already too big." "Why won't you straighten your hair? Nobody wants to see curly, nappy hair." Yet, as a child, you always stayed true to you. I admired that about you. You never conformed to anyone else's way of being. You stood headstrong in your beliefs, in your individuality, and in your uniqueness.

Somewhere along the journey, that changed. You started to believe that being who you are is not enough. You started to believe the projections of others, and you began to dim your light for others. Only to find yourself lost, confused, and ultimately needing solitude to find you again. I admire your strength. Though you lost

136

yourself along the way, you never gave up on finding you again. Maybe not the previous version, but the new and improved one.

You kept fighting for your truth. You realized that there is no need for validation outside of self. You are who you are and that is enough. That is what makes you, you. That is what makes us, us. Never feel bad for being who you are. Never allow anyone else to project that who you are is not beautiful, as you are. As we are. Inside and out. Every version on you is beautiful. No matter what mistakes you've made, you are and always have been and always will be, ENOUGH. I love you.

The Mind. The Body. The Word.

"In the beginning was the Word, and the word was with God, and the Word was God." John 1:1

Prayer is simply words filled with intention. There is no distinct way to pray. God asks that as we speak, we use our word with intention. Bringing forth only what we truly desire to be manifested in truth and reality. God is love, wholeness, infinite waters of abundance that flows eternally, at no halt. A fairness. A truth. Prosperity, in all things.

Your word is your bond and your word is everlasting. Your words are extremely powerful. What you speak over your life becomes a covenant with spirit, with self, with the Universe. That is why it is extremely important to be impeccable with your words. Your voice IS power! You hold the power to create life, and death, in all things. Choose your words wisely.

Use them with the intention to evolve and curate a space, a frequency, a divine union of love and unity in all things. Utilize your words to empower, not deny. Your words can and will be the changing factor of your life. Time and space are infinite, but so are your words. They send ripple effects through the earth's core. Make sure the vibrations your words emit are one that uplift and inspire, not degrade and belittle.

I know throughout childhood; you battled with the opinions of others. The naysayers, the ones that used their words as swords. However, I encourage you to learn from their mistakes. How those words made you feel not only impacted you, but they impacted your ancestors, the population, as well as your children to come. We are all connected. You have the ability to choose whether you carry the burden of false statements, projections of other's insecurities, and outdated ways of thinking with you on your journey. OR you could decide to curate a new story.

138

Be the author of your own book. Decide to change the narrative, use your words with intention and speak life over yourself, your lineage, and even your pain. Their words do not have to be your truth. Their projections, insecurities, moments of belittlement, are not who you are. They reflect who they are. Speak life over yourself. Do not joke or play around with your words. Your brain cannot tell the difference between a joke and truth. Your mind believes what you tell it, so tell it beautiful things.

Before word, there is thought. In thought lies the first step to manifestation. Your thoughts become words and in turn become physical manifestations. That is why it is imperative to consciously curate your thoughts. Your thoughts send out vibrations as well. They ripple into the universe, into the cosmos, but most importantly, into your subconscious mind.

Your subconscious mind believes what you think and what you say, no matter what it is. So, even if you are struggling to believe in good things, tell them to yourself anyway. Eventually, you will begin to believe them because energy is energy. It has to align. If you are speaking beautiful things over yourself, your life, the ones you love, then only beautiful things will manifest. Don't overthink it.

Allow yourself to shift easily and abundantly. "I am enough," doesn't need a follow up question or thought. It is what it is. As in that, so are all thoughts. They simply are what they are. Energy, frequency, alignment. You get to decide what you want to align with. You choose if you want to lead with a high vibrational charge on the Universe, on self, on Spirit.

The Word is God. The Word is Source. The Word is love. You are of God; therefore, you are the abundance, the love, the joy, the peace, the calm, the faithfulness, the kindness, and the fulfillment you seek. It was, never has been, and never will be outside of you. It is within. God is within.

You hold everything you have been searching for. As you journey through life, there will be people that project their opinions, thoughts, and feelings onto you. You will see and hear things that aren't the kindest things, but what you must come to understand is YOU decide what your truth is. The words YOU speak, the words YOU believe, and the love YOU create is what becomes your truth. I encourage you to speak LIFE in all things and over all things.

Engulf yourself in the brilliance of Spirit, in the abundance of love that is God. Create in, and out of, a space of authenticity, purity, joy, kindness, truth, but most importantly, love. Your words are important. Your voice matters. Never allow anyone or anything to silence you. Never allow anyone or anything to make you feel as though your voice does not matter. You are purposeful and so is your word. I love you.

Forgiveness

"Forgiveness clears my path" -Bossy Bruja

Forgiveness is not about forgetting, Forgiveness is about liberation. It is the moment you decide that you will no longer carry the weight of other people's pain as your own. It's the moment you stop allowing your past to speak louder than your present. You forgive, not as an excuse or an "it's okay," but to release. And in that release, you find your liberation. Forgiveness can be a bridge that leads you back to yourself.

It is the embodiment of no longer needing to replay betrayals or rehearse pain as a way to justify the wrongs you've experienced. We can choose lightness over lingering in the shadows. In making the decision to liberate ourselves, we find true peace.

WE find true freedom. Free to love without walls. Free to create without fear. Free to walk in our purpose without the chains of resentment or regret. Every time we forgive, a burden slips off our shoulders and makes our journey a little less heavy. A layer of shame is dissolved. A deeper breath is returned. Forgiveness allows us to meet ourselves again—whole, healed, cleansed, renewed, and pure. Forgiveness is the highest act of love one can exhibit.

I want you to know, it is okay for you, for us, to still be learning how to forgive. You've carried guilt for staying too long, trusting too quickly, and giving too much of yourself away. You beat yourself up for the moments you ignored your intuition, quieted your voice of inner knowing— the one that tried to whisper, "This isn't safe. This doesn't feel right." But now, I see you clearly. You weren't weak. You weren't naïve. You were hopeful. Loving. Trying your best with the tools you had at your disposal and the heart you carried. I forgive you.

Forgiving ourselves is one of the most important parts of this journey because we have to be willing to release the burdens of the past. We have to be willing to release the burdens of decisions we made from a space when we didn't know better. I forgive you for not knowing how to protect yourself in spaces you were never meant to be in. I forgive you for the silence you kept to survive. I forgive you for every time you thought someone else's treatment of you was a reflection of your worth, of our worth.

You didn't deserve the hurt, but you also don't deserve to carry the shame for how you coped with it. So, I'm letting it go now—bit by bit, breath by breath, tear by tear, day by day. Not to erase what happened, but to set you free from the stories it left behind. To assist you in putting the pieces of you that were left torn, broken, shattered, wounded, and disregarded back together.

Forgiveness won't come overnight, and I am not forcing it. However, I am choosing, every day, to give you peace where others gave you pain. And if I ever forget that... please forgive me. Know that I am doing my absolutely best to create a safe space filled with love and reassurance within us. I promise to keep loving you. I promise to always protect you. I promise to always remind you that you were never the problem.

Forgiveness does not invalidate your pain. It is not synonymous with allowing those who have hurt you back in. It simply means, we are no longer allowing ourselves to be weighed down by the projections and actions of those who have hurt us. Forgiveness is a journey. I won't rush you to forgive. I won't gaslight you into pretending it didn't hurt. Instead, I will walk with you. I'll sit with you. I'll sit with the anger, the heartbreak, the aching questions. Little by little, we will loosen the grip they still have on us, FOR US. Because you deserve peace. We deserve peace. You deserve a life where their actions don't echo in every relationship, every moment of joy, or every quiet night. You deserve to feel whole... even if the apologies never come.

From this day forth, I promise to do the work to fill those spaces that were left opened. I can't promise you that I will never make another mistake or that we will never be hurt again, but what I can promise you is I will forever be your friend. I will always love you to the best of my ability. I will be that safe space when you need me. I will do the things that bring you joy. I will always show you love. I promise to reclaim our power. I am choosing to take the initiative to give us the freedom we deserve. I love you.

"Trust your journey." -Yinessa Nicole

Now that I have arrived to this place of knowing, I see that each experience—no matter how painful—was leading me back home to myself. Every misstep, every heartbreak, every mistake, every moment I thought I wouldn't make it... it was a portal. A portal into a version of self that I would have never known, or met, had I not experienced all I have experienced. It was all a gateway to the woman I have now become. I no longer look at my younger self with sadness or regret. I see her as a warrior in bloom. She didn't need to be fixed. She simply needed to be loved, held, nurtured, cared for, and told the truth: that she was NEVER broken to begin with.

Understanding my worth has given me permission to stop striving to be chosen. I have chosen to choose myself. I have chosen to validate myself. In that choice, I have unlocked a deep, unshakable love that no external validation could ever match. My mind is no longer a battlefield. It is a sanctuary. A sacred space filled with words of affirmation, peace, and clarity. My body is no longer a place I escape. It is MY temple—my holy ground. And my words? They are no longer laced with apology, shame, or fear. They are divine incantations of liberation, curated with love, woven with intention, and backed by Spirit.

Forgiveness has set me free. Not just from others and their opinions, persecution, lies, and projections, but from the noose I used to have around my own neck. I've forgiven myself for not knowing better. For dimming my own light for the comfortability of others. For being human. That forgiveness has softened me. And in my new, profound, softness, I've discovered an entirely new strength. One that doesn't need to be loud to be felt. One that doesn't need to prove itself to be powerful. It is. I am. Whole.

To my younger self, baby girl, I love you. You are so special. You always have been, and you always will be. You are THAT GIRL. I love you with a depth I didn't know was possible. You did everything you could with the tools you had. You weren't weak for surviving, sweetheart, you were DIVINE! You held on when you had every reason to let go. You protected your joy the best way you knew how. And now, I carry that joy with reverence. I vow to always protect it. I vow to always protect you... to protect our crown. One we have earned through fortitude and righteousness even in times of adversity.

You can rest now. You don't have to be in survival mode anymore. You are safe here, with me. You are allowed to laugh fully, cry freely, dream wildly, and love deeply. I am giving you everything you were once denied, and I am doing it without conditions. You don't have to earn my love. You already have it.

To my present self, young woman, I am so damn proud of you. You have taken everything meant to destroy you and turned it into medicine. You have created beauty from your bruises and poetry from your pain. You speak up for yourself with grace. You take up space. You are no longer shrinking yourself to make others comfortable. You are expanding, radiating, exploring, and showing others what is possible when a woman chooses herself

146

fully. The journey hasn't been perfect, but it has been perfectly imperfect for you. You set boundaries with grace. You walk away from what is no longer serving you. Not out of bitterness, but from deep self-respect.

I see how gentle you are with your heart now. How you've made peace your priority and made peace with your pain. I want you to know, you are doing a phenomenal job. You are exactly where you are meant to be, doing exactly what you should be doing, and going exactly where you should be going.

To the version of me I have yet to meet, I am excited to become you. I will keep tending to this inner garden. I will keep shedding and growing. I will continue listening to my intuition and walking in my truth. I will continue choosing softness in a world that does all it can to harden you. I will keep showing up for us, day in and day out.

This letter isn't just a reflection, but a promise. A vow to never abandon myself again. A declaration that I am worthy, whole, and divinely guided. I am not my past. I am the author of my future. This time, the story ends in healing, freedom, and joy. Perseverance is my power, and I choose to do it with ease.

With love,
Mauryunna N. Brown (Me).

Help Is Human

By Meisha Pon

Dear Black woman,
If no one has told you lately, hear this now:

It's OK to ask for help.
If the help doesn't come, it does not mean you are undeserving.

Oh, how I wish I had heard these words
and truly learned this lesson
as a young girl.

It is OK to ask for help.

Instead, I interpreted every unmet request as unworthiness starting in childhood into adulthood. I wore unworthiness as a label and like a second skin.

With each unmet need, I built invisible walls to shield myself from the sting of disappointment. Layer upon layer, I constructed a fortress to keep pain out. But the thicker the walls became, the heavier it felt to carry them. I ended up barricading myself inside a life that looked functional, but felt isolating, and so very lonely.

I became afraid to ask for help.
Afraid, no one would listen.
Afraid, no one would care.

Asking for help felt like sitting through a sandstorm with no shelter. Bare-skinned and vulnerable while the wind whipped every grain of silence and indifference against me. I stood there, unseen, while others walked by, unaware of the storm raging inside of me.

It was a storm only I could feel. But its sting left lasting marks.

In time, I lost the ability to even know what I wanted.
To feel the truth of my own needs.

I couldn't name them.
I couldn't ask for them.
I couldn't believe I was deserving of them.

So, I downplayed my needs.
Buried them so deep, I dismissed myself.
I prioritized others to the point that I no longer recognized the woman I was becoming.

I became a shell of myself. A shapeshifter
Flowing like the breeze.
Molding myself into whatever others needed me to
be.
Attaching myself to their opinions and calling them
my own.

I smiled when I wanted to scream.
I agreed when I didn't.
I laughed at things that hurt deeply.

Little by little, I traded authenticity for acceptance.

Dear Black girl,
Let me tell you something true:
Your environment does not define you.

Yes, it shapes you.
Yes, it influences you.
But it is not the total sum of you.

There is a deeper you.
A you beyond what you were told.

Use your curiosity to rediscover her.
Let it guide you to your voice, your fears, your
wonder.

You have permission to feel
The rage. The sadness. The joy. The awe. The
disappointment.

Feel it all.
Your emotions are not too much.
They are evidence that you are alive, human, and
whole.

And your tears?
They are not a weakness.
Embrace them because they are the gateway to a
more grounded, resolute you.

Please, understand your caregivers may not have
met your needs, but that doesn't mean your needs
weren't real. Feel the hurt and hold them
accountable.

Know this:

They did the best they could with what they had.
And they couldn't give what they never received.
They were often surviving, not feeling.
They wore silence like armor too.

So, when you cried, they may have handed you quiet. When you asked, they may have taught you not to need.

Their lack of expression was not a reflection of your worth.

Extend them grace and while you're at it, return that grace to yourself.

You are not "too much" because you long for:
A warm embrace.
Gentle words of affirmation.
Emotional safety.
Consistent displays of love.

You are not too much.

Your desire for love does not make you needy.
It makes you human.

You are worthy!

And listen,
Because you didn't feel loved as a child
doesn't mean love wasn't present.

Love can be quiet.
It can be broken.
It can be buried under fear or trauma or the
unspoken.

People love in different ways, often limited by what
they were taught.
But hear this clearly:
Having unmet needs does not make you unlovable,
unworthy, or undeserving.

Your unmet needs have no ties to your value.

You are worthy.
You are beauty itself.

Forgive the men who betrayed your trust—

the men who hurt you when you were most
vulnerable,

who took advantage of you in ways that left deep
wounds.

You do not have to carry their actions as your
identity.

Your healing is not about excusing them.

It is about choosing freedom for yourself.

And that freedom? It begins when you reclaim your voice.

Know that your strength lies in your voice, and your truth.

Speak up; do not suffer in silence.

You are worthy!

It's easy to seek validation from your environment
But true healing starts when you learn to validate yourself.

Look at the obstacles you've overcome.
The pain you've survived.
The stories you've rewritten.

Each one holds wisdom.
Each one is a reminder:
You are resilient.
You are courageous.
You know how to begin again.

Celebrate your redirections.

Honor the moments you chose differently.

They are breadcrumbs leading you back to you.

And yes,

Because you know how to fight

does not mean you are meant to live in battle.

That armor you built to protect yourself?

You don't have to wear it forever.

Remove it, piece by piece.

With each layer you shed, you will find

freedom of expression,

relief,

joy,

acceptance.

That armor is lined with stories you once told

yourself to survive.

Some of those stories were never true.

Some have expired.

Revising those stories gives your body the chance to

catch up with your spirit.

To catch up with your actual age.

Spend time with yourself.
In the quiet is where your truth will meet you.

Finding yourself is like uncovering your favorite candy unwrapped and forgotten, buried beneath a rug, covered in lint.

You don't even remember how it got there.
But you do remember the joy it once brought you.

The flavor.
The texture.
The delight.

You pick it up, and you take the time to clean it.
Because underneath the dust, the sweetness is still intact.

You remember what made you fall in love with it in the first place.
That's what reclaiming yourself feels like.
You were never lost.
Just hidden.
Just waiting.

Oh, all the places you'll go when you learn to trust yourself.

You are equipped to hear and listen to your inner voice.

You are capable of meeting the parts of you still entangled in fear.

You are deserving of immersion in your own beauty.

Your self-worth is an expression of your self-love.
And your love is not conditional.
It is enduring.

And don't forget:
All you can do is your best.

And your best?
It changes.
With time.
With wisdom.
With softness.

What is true today may not be true tomorrow
and that's OK.

You are more than capable.

You are perfectly imperfect.

You are worthy of support.

Asking for help makes you human.

Give yourself permission to not walk alone.

With love,
Meisha

Re-Mothering Myself

By Mika Dean Newton

Dear Little Me,

Hey baby girl.

I see you.

I see that little brown girl sitting in silence with so much held inside, trying to make sense of a world that asked you to grow up faster than it should have. You learned early how to keep things together, how to be "good," how to be helpful, how to be invisible when the house needed stillness. You didn't speak unless necessary. You made yourself small before anyone asked you to. And somehow, the world praised you for it.

You were only seven when you began caring for your little brother.

He was four—wide-eyed and curious, always looking to you for guidance, laughter, or comfort. You weren't his mother, but you were something sacred to him. You were stability. You were routine. You were the warm body in the room when the night stretched long and lonely. You figured out how to hold space for him, how to calm him, how to

161

distract him, how to entertain him without ever raising your voice. Because raising your voice? That wasn't allowed.

At night, while Mommy worked, the two of you were home alone. You didn't feel like a child then. You felt like a quiet protector. You locked the doors. You kept the lights on. You pretended not to be scared even when the shadows felt too big. You didn't cry. You just stayed still. You knew how to do that. During the day, when Mommy slept, you kept that same silence. Tiptoes. Whispers. No music. No noise. You carried your needs like secrets, small and hidden.

Your mother worked hard. She loved you, but she didn't always show it the way you needed. She was tired. She was heartbroken. She was battling her own depression and fighting wars inside herself that you didn't understand. You only knew that sometimes she was distant, other times short, sometimes mean—and you never knew which version of her you were going to get. You and your brother learned to play rock-paper-scissors to decide who had to knock on the door and ask her for food, for water, for anything. Because even the smallest requests felt like they were too much.

You missed her even when she was right there.

There were Christmases you didn't see her. You thought she chose to work the holiday for the extra pay. It wasn't until much later that you learned she probably didn't have a choice. But that didn't soften the ache. That didn't change the fact that her absence left a quiet hollowness under the tree. Your grandparents and aunts tried to fill the gap. They made the holidays magical, overcompensating with food and laughter and gifts. And you were grateful. But a part of you still waited for her. A part of you always waited.

And yet—there was love.

Your aunts and grandmother gave you softness. They gave you gentleness. They gave you what your mother couldn't. They braided your hair slowly, told you stories, made you feel pretty, special, and safe. They nurtured you. And it was through them that you began to understand what it meant to be held. To be poured into. You tucked that love away like

163

medicine, knowing that one day you would use it to heal someone else.

You grew up fast. You had a childhood, but you were always aware. Always mature. Always worried. Anxiety found you early, though you didn't know its name back then. You were just always thinking. Always planning. Always trying to be prepared. You figured out how to do your own homework, how to take care of your brother, how to apply to college. You read the fine print. You made the calls. You filled out the forms. You became your own guidance counselor, your own tutor, your own cheerleader.

And somewhere in the middle of all that survival, you learned to perform.

You learned that good grades made people proud of you. That being smart got you attention. That being well-behaved made adults smile. So, you performed. You wore achievement like armor. You smiled through confusion. You didn't ask for help. You didn't raise your hand—even when you knew the answer. You didn't want to be "too much." You didn't want to draw attention. You didn't want to risk being wrong. So, you kept shrinking. Not just in the classroom, but everywhere.

You shrank in friendships. You didn't speak up when someone hurt your feelings. You laughed off things that weren't funny. You let people talk over you.

You shrank in relationships. You made yourself easier to love. More agreeable. Less opinionated. You became what you thought they wanted. You stayed when you should've walked. You chased love that didn't chase you back. You gave everything and asked for little. You tried to prove your worth through patience, through sex, through sacrifice.

You shrank at work. You did extra without credit. You held your tongue in meetings. You downplayed your gifts. You let others take the spotlight even when you built the stage.

Because speaking up felt dangerous.

Because silence had kept you safe.

Your father was in and out of your life. You loved him. He loved you too—in his own broken way. But he was battling addiction. And addiction is a thief. It stole his consistency. It stole your trust. It stole your sense of stability. Sometimes he showed up and laughed with you. Other times he disappeared or left you with your stepmother and sisters while he vanished. You didn't wait on porches for him. But you did wait. For calls. For attention. For effort.

You were angry. At him. At your mother. But you didn't say it. You dared not say it. You buried that anger deep. You told yourself to be understanding. To be grateful. To be mature. But the truth is—your childhood had cracks in it. Beautiful in places, yes. But broken in others. And the silence you were raised in became the silence you carried.

But you never stayed stuck.

Even in your quietest seasons, something in you refused to disappear.

You started finding your voice. Slowly. Tentatively. Then fiercely.

You started saying no. You started speaking up. You started asking for what you needed. You started telling the truth—your truth—not just the version that made everyone else comfortable. You stopped letting people walk all over you. You stopped shrinking in rooms that couldn't hold your fullness. You stopped performing.

And then—you became a mother.

And something cracked open.

Your daughter became your reason and your reflection. Through her, you saw the little girl you once were. You made a vow—one you've kept every day since: she would know love. She would know safety. She would know that her voice matters. That her tears are welcome. That her joy is sacred. That her boundaries will be honored.

You mothered her the way you wished you'd been mothered.

You held her with softness. You looked her in the eyes when she spoke. You celebrated her curiosity. You never demanded her silence. You let her be free. And in loving her, you began re-mothering yourself.

You held your inner child close and whispered to her:

"You didn't deserve to carry all of that alone."
"You don't have to be perfect to be loved."
"You can rest now."
"You are allowed to take up space."
"You were always enough."

You started healing the parts of you that had gone quiet for too long. You started pouring love into the corners of your spirit that had gone untouched. You started grieving the childhood you didn't fully get. And then—you started reclaiming.

You are reclaiming your voice.
Reclaiming your presence.
Reclaiming your body.
Reclaiming your rest.
Reclaiming your softness.
Reclaiming your power.
Reclaiming your right to take up space.
Reclaiming your right to speak up.
Reclaiming the joy you postponed.
Reclaiming the rage you swallowed.

Reclaiming the brilliance you dimmed.

Reclaiming the life you thought you had to earn.

You are reclaiming the girl who knew the answers but kept her hand down.

The teen who laughed quietly so no one noticed her pain.

The woman who tried to become everything for everyone else.

The healer who finally became everything for herself.

You are reclaiming your story.

Your laughter.

Your sound.

Your rhythm.

Your boundaries.

Your sacred "no."

Your glorious "yes."

You became a healer—not just in name, but in being. You hold space for other women to find their voices. You guide them back to their rest. You help them feel seen, heard, whole. You are the lighthouse now. You are the soft place. You are the sound. The truth. The permission.

169

And I am so proud of you.

Proud of the way you kept going.
Proud of the way you loved, even when love felt
uncertain.
Proud of the way you protected your brother.
Proud of the way you forgave your parents.
Proud of the way you parented your daughter.
Proud of the way you chose yourself—again and
again and again.

You are the one who broke the cycle.
You are the one who healed the lineage.
You are the one who came home to herself.

And baby girl, you didn't just find your voice.
You found your power.
You found your peace.
You found your way.

I love you.
I honor you.
I will never abandon you again.

You are home.
You are whole.
You are free.

With everything in me,
Mika (Me)

I
Fought
for Me

By Nikki Shantell

"Get my baby! Get my baby!" The words my mother screamed as she realized that I had jumped in the swimming pool at the early age of three. I've always remembered this moment. I remember my older sister (13 at the time) was swimming, so I decided to jump in the pool, smiling as I was going down. My sister was the one who jumped back in to save me. Yet, I wasn't scared. My mom and sister said I laughed when I came out. I don't remember anything after jumping in and smiling.

It's a prelude to my life pattern. To our life pattern. As an adult, I now realize that this moment is what shaped me, because it showed me what I am capable of. That jump in the pool at three led me to being a self-taught swimmer by the age of five. That jump at three has allowed me to move thousands of miles away from home to live and work in South Korea as well as the U.S. Virgin Islands. That jump at three has allowed me to leave jobs and people who no longer serve me. Serve is not used in a selfish way, but in terms of not treating me properly, whether it is financially, physically, or emotionally. That jump allowed me to be bold, take chances, and deal with the what-ifs later.

Trauma walks with you

"I wish there was a perfect scenario where I could
state that my negative experiences didn't affect: my
perspective on life, how I respond to things, or how I
even viewed myself."

As a kid, witnessing domestic violence amongst
your parents is one of the toughest things to see.
Though the time has long passed, it has left
remnants of the broken pieces. Not only was seeing
it hard but having to deal with the feelings that come
along with it as a child trying to figure out how to
navigate those feelings. I was a daddy's girl. But
being a daddy's girl doesn't mean I don't love my
mom. So, I never wanted to see my mom cry or
hurt. One morning, I remember waking up and my
brother and I were looking around and we asked my
mom where Dad went. And I don't remember her
answer, but I remember walking around the house
and opening up the closet door and noticing that my
dad's stuff was gone.

As a child, I didn't understand what was going on
and how that would affect me and had affected me.
That feeling of abandonment had carried over into

my adult life. From a psychological point of view, early childhood abandonment can lead to perfectionism because the child learns that being perfect might prevent them from being rejected or left again. The child strives for flawlessness to feel worthy of love and security.

It gives you a feeling of you have to do things right, you have to be perfect. You can't upset a person who you care about because if you do that, it's going to cause them to leave, and the last thing that we want is for someone to leave us. Going through my teens, 20s, all the way up until my mid-30s, I was a people pleaser. It took a mental breakdown and physical injury for me to finally come to a point where I realized trying to please others is never going to get them to stay. Trying to please others will never make someone treat me how I deserve to be treated. Trying to please others will not bring me peace. Instead, being a people pleaser causes stress, anxiety, and confusion.

Now I understand that the people that are meant to be in your life will actively be in your life. Anyone that chooses to leave, whether by deciding to walk away or having to disassociate myself with them

175

based on how they have mistreated me, should be considered a season experience.

Have No Regrets

"Regret is a thing that really stings."

Many people may say they don't have any regrets, spending so much time trying to escape mentally. As we continue to try to escape mentally, as the days, weeks, months, and years pass us by, we have found a way to convince ourselves that whatever that thing was that happened to us, it didn't happen. It wasn't worth it. It's not a big deal. We try to minimize that negative thing as much as you possibly can in order to forget about it.

I was sexually assaulted in college and never really told anyone, yet I live with that feeling every day. There is a ball of anxiety that I experience when I think about how I should have spoken up. Going to a college gathering and becoming intoxicated, thinking I am amongst friends. Someone was supposed to drive me home, only to find out you're in the back room by yourself and your friend, the person that was supposed to drive you home, had left because somebody told them that somebody else was going to drive you home. Only for you to be on your cycle and to be sexually assaulted in the home of the offender, after constantly telling this offender no. The most traumatic part of it is, you never say anything because who's going to believe you, right? You were drunk—why were you drunk? How dare you be a 21-year-old student in college and you're intoxicated? This is because society has conditioned the people to turn on the victims instead of speaking up and out against the offenders.

Self-advocacy is one of the strongest powers you will have. It's your own voice that has to speak up and out. It may seem scary, you may be uncertain, you may even think you are trying to protect others, but who is protecting you? No matter what, speak up for YOU.

Grief Has No Expiration

"Life is for the living. Death is for the dead. Let life be like music, and death a note unsaid." — Langston Hughes

Losing a loved one is not something that ever becomes easy. The saying that time heals all wounds is not something that makes sense in the real world. Time will surely pass by, but that doesn't keep your mind from forgetting. At some point in life, we realize that when we were younger, we didn't attend as many funerals. Unfortunately, we do have situations where we lose loved ones at an extremely young age. But, the older we become, the more death we experience. And the closer we are to the loved ones who we are losing, the less we feel good about moving on in life. It says, though we can no longer be happy. Not because there isn't anything that will make us happy, but because we don't feel it's fair to be able to be happy and move on with life, knowing that we have people who could no longer be here with us to experience the same thing. I've lost grandparents, aunts, uncles, cousins, and friends. I still remember their faces. I still remember their names. I still remember the love that was displayed, and I still cry. One of the deaths that I took the hardest was the passing of my stepdad. It caused me to question God. It caused me to lose faith in God. It caused me to even consider changing religions. But my stepdad himself was a man of God.

A man who would religiously sit down and read his Bible. So when he received the news from his doctors that he was only going to live for a certain amount of time, he was in a good place mentally. He was okay with what was going to happen, and he tried to prepare our family to be okay with it. But regardless of how much we know that there's a cycle of life, and that cycle always ends with death, it never makes the grief any better. Now, I hold on and rejoice in visits from ancestors. Those dreams that we have out of nowhere—but a simple reminder that they are always with us.

You can also take grief a step further to understand that it also encompasses grieving the loss of a friendship, the loss of a relationship, or the loss of self.

The biggest lesson hit after getting a divorce. I never thought that I would end up divorced because I was so in love, we were so in love. I remember the judge telling us that we were young and that we would marry someone else, but all I could think about was that I didn't want to remarry. I wanted my husband. I wanted what we had to work. I now understand that marriage is a combination of two people, who

179

more than likely have both experienced trauma in some capacity, coming together as one. If that childhood trauma is not addressed, it comes out in various ways. Trauma can cause your response and perception of a person to differ from another.

Nonetheless, the divorce was finalized. This grief process couldn't have come at a worse time. It came at a time when I was already forced to sit down, so now I was forced to think out everything, to feel every single emotion. So now, not only am I grieving a marriage that has dismantled, but also the person who I was. My identity at this point had been stripped. I was no longer a wife. I was no longer an officer. I was no longer a healthy individual. I was no longer an athlete. I was just… who was I? I needed God more than ever.

Inside Job

"Being in a peaceful state of mind is an inside job."

The toughest thing that I had to endure in my life was an injury that affected my breathing, which in turn affected my entire life. This injury changed everything about me. I was accustomed to being physically fit, working out 5 to 7 days out of the week, playing basketball, taking solo trips, and being able to do whatever I wanted to do—to being unable to breathe on a daily basis. Not only was I physically battling with what my body was enduring, but also there was a mental battle that was worse than the physical challenges that I was dealing with. When we don't want to deal with something, we find ways to occupy our time in order to get it out of our mind. It is hard as a human being to have to sit in the midst of the storm while trying to heal at the same time. The healing that I had to endure was an active healing. While I was going through everything that I was going through, my mind became my worst enemy.

Your people, your true tribe, will be there for you no matter what. My family and my friends were a lot of help for me. My family has helped tremendously, whether financially, emotionally, or physically, as there were so many things that I couldn't do for myself. One thing they couldn't do is remove my pain and take the depression away. Now this part is where it gets tough. I've thought in the past that I had hit my lowest in life, but this was the lowest. I'm in pain, broke and broken. How is it possible to go from having your dream career, that took you almost three years to obtain, to having to medically retire? All while fighting to be heard! Fighting the doctors at one point to believe me. I remember sitting in a doctor's office telling the doctor what happens to me. I could tell by how he looked that he didn't believe me. Then he sees with his own eyes what happens, and his eyes became so big.

I have a feeling I will one day get closer, health-wise, to my previous self. However, who I am mentally and emotionally was created through a story of faith. Throughout numerous years of my life, there have been times that I felt the need to drastically drop down to my knees and cry out loud to speak to God. These moments are huge moments for me—huge decisions, scary decisions, hurt, and so much more. But none of those things compared to me having to fully let go of any idea of control and ask God to please carry me as I am not strong enough to walk. This ask was not a one-time ask. It went on for months. The magnitude of pain, trauma, stress, and fear weighed on me extremely heavily. No amount of love from my family or friends could bring me out of this dark pit. It was nothing that they could do to help me feel safe or secure, nor confident about everything that I was experiencing.

Pressure bursts pipes.

"Not everything that is faced can be changed, but nothing can be changed until it is faced." — James Baldwin

The roller coaster ride of life has been extremely interesting. I actually thought when my injury initially happened that I was going to be back to my normal self. I never anticipated being out of work for 30 days, let alone having to retire early in this way. As usual, life happens, but I never expected any of this. I had a plan. I am the person who always has a plan, as I like to have some type of organization, some control. My plan: get a government job, travel with that government job, retire 20 years from my start date. God had similar plans, but I consider God's plans were drastically different from my own.

This particular trauma isn't something that is a quick fix. I was going through the 12 steps of grief on a continuous cycle, never reaching a point of relief, acceptance, or resolution. How could I feel calm and at peace when my body is fighting overtime? How could I achieve acceptance when this was no fault of my own and I'm reminded daily of my loss?

I had to begin seeing a therapist on a regular basis because I was a wreck. There were many days and nights I spent lying on the floor inside of my closet, crying because I was physically tired and drained mentally and financially. My body had been fighting for itself at this point continuously. I've been fighting doctors to be heard, government agencies to be heard, and was regularly at a doctor's office. It took a toll on my overall health. There were endless sleepless nights and a fear that I wouldn't wake up in the morning. It was a heavy load to bear. I got to a point where I thought it would be easier to just no longer be. Suicide crossed my mind on multiple occasions, but the one thing that kept me were the thoughts of my nieces and nephews. I can hold on for my babies.

Manifesting and spiritual awakening

"When you have exhausted all possibilities, remember this — you haven't." — Thomas Edison

As a child, I would always journal. Journaling and reading were always therapeutic for me. I would journal everything—how I felt, what I did, what I wanted, and so much more. One day, while visiting my mother at her home, I found an old journal entry that I wrote. This particular entry was about my future luxuries, or what a high school student may have considered a luxury. As I reviewed the list, I realized that I obtained some of those items that were listed. I had no idea that as an adult, I would continue the same process of journaling and manifesting. We may call it different things— manifesting or praying—but whatever you call it, it all boils down to believing that particular thing will find you.

Years after my injury, one day I decided to try again. I decided this time to concentrate on the things I could control only. I started making small changes, such as speaking more positively to myself, praying more, dressing up when I go out, walking with correct posture, and smiling more. I changed the way I ate since I became unable to work out how I was accustomed to, or even on a beginner level. The biggest change was me having faith that God was

185

working in my favor. Even though I could not see the future or understand the reason why, I can have unwavering faith. I then noticed things started to change around me. The things that I started to speak over my life and write out for my future were happening. I had to understand that this has all been bigger than me. God was demanding my attention.

Victory is mine

"Some things are a battle, but I'm war ready."

It took me a few battles to figure it out, but I now know my story will always end in victory. My name translates to victory of people, and this is no coincidence. My bloodline is full of beautiful women who are and were fighters. Women who were placed in life situations that could have broken them. Instead, they found strength in their struggle. I am equipped with everything I need in order to solve any problems that will come my way, which includes having the right people by my side. It is your choice to pick those who have access to you and what type of access.

My favorite quote is: *"There are years that ask questions, and years that answer." — Zora Neale Hurston*

I view this quote as something taking place in one's life that they are questioning—why me? When will? How will? Then, there is a season of "this is the reason." That season of answers feels good. However, we must know how to navigate both seasons of ups and downs.

2005, 2007, 2008, 2010, 2016, 2017, 2019, 2021, 2022, and 2023. These are all of the years in my adult life that I had a season of something negative. Within these years, I asked, why me? The turmoil may not have lasted the entire year, but I remember saying this is the worst year. In hindsight, some of the situations were minute in comparison to my last three years. Nonetheless, I have continued to persevere through all obstacles over the years.

Things to remember:

- Be kind to yourself
- It's OK to cry
- Give yourself grace

- Every little step matters
- Seasons change
- Self-care is not selfish
- Learn when to pivot

Wishing you love and positivity!
Nikki S.

Speak, Little Me

By Robin Blue

Somewhere between innocence and silence, a little girl began to disappear. Not because she wanted to—but because the world kept taking pieces of her without permission. They stole moments she couldn't name, whispered things she didn't understand, and left her to carry secrets that never belonged to her. But today, the silence ends. Today, I write to that girl and tell her: I see you. I remember. And I've come to set you free.

Dear Little Me,

I see you. Yes, you, the one dancing in her room with her own shadow. The bright-eyed, imaginative, curious little girl, I see you in the quiet moments, where you sit wondering what life, beyond what you know, could be. I see you jumping between hopscotch and single rope, as if the world feels safe, just for a moment. I see you in the stolen minutes of daydreaming. I see you in the strength you don't even know you have yet—the determination to push forward even when the world around you tries to steal your innocence and silence your spirit. I see you, and I honor you.

Hey there. Hear me well, you are doing nothing wrong. You don't deserve what is happening to you. You are a child, beautiful, innocent, and trusting. You didn't invite it. You didn't cause it. Please understand you were never at fault. Your light was never the problem. Someone took advantage of your light.

There's a tiny soldier in you, surviving when you should only be dreaming.

. In kindergarten, when you should have been drawing daisy pictures and eating egg salad sandwiches from a cartoon lunch box, they were indoctrinating you and causing that garden to bloom way too soon. You were trying to be a child, living, laughing, and growing. You believed and trusted people who were left to care for you. They knew what they were doing was wrong. They confused your cuteness with sexiness. But hear me, Smoke — a nickname only a few understood - you were brave even when you didn't know the words for what was happening. Abuse and trauma are not in your vocabulary yet. You don't know the damage or the difference. Your innocence doesn't see the

191

inappropriateness of being touched, held, kissed, or misused by grown men.

Sometimes our bodies can betray us, leading us to believe that what we feel feels good. So why not allow it to happen? Later, you will realize it is inappropriate and how dare they violate you in such a way. Innocence doesn't fade—it's stolen slowly and way too soon.

But before healing can begin, the truth must be spoken—no matter how much it tumbles between your stomach and the back of your throat.

I know you believe it is truly a secret and an innocent one. They have convinced you not to tell anybody about it. That would violate your special friendship. Sharing your 'special times' would cause others to look at them differently. If it's such a good thing, then maybe others should know.

These people are supposed to be responsible for you, love you, and care for you. It's OK! Tell your story even if your voice shakes; even if you don't know what words to say, even if you are afraid. I want you to know it's okay to name what's happening.

Share this experience with the ones you love, as it should, but it's OK if you don't. I acknowledge the pain you face in holding information that should be released. I encourage you to speak up. Even if you stumble with your words, tell God in your prayers. He can start opening the door and let the truth come out. If you must, whisper until someone listens.

To keep silent only protects the abuser. Understand that your voice is your power, even if it trembles. Your voice is your strength; people hear and listen when you use it. But if you don't use your control, if you don't speak, don't tell it, it will continue. It provides cover for the people who stole your innocence.

It leaves you confused about what truth is and unaware of what love is. God loves you. I love you. Your story matters. You matter. You are loved. You are cherished. You are essential, and there's life ahead of you. You have a mission in life. Your silence can abort that mission. Let your voice be heard.

When we finally name it, we can begin to forgive—not for them, but to free ourselves. I can't tell you to forget it; however, you must at least forgive it. You don't know now, but forgiving yourself is more important than anything else you can do.

That is trauma. Trauma can steal your sense of control. Call it icky, if you must. Say it … That is abuse. That is wrong.

It's been more than 5 years now. Silence has had its season, but silence never saved me. The garden didn't just grow wild; it grew without protectors. And now, the one left to fend for herself is rising to guard it. No longer wait to be rescued. Reclaim every root.

No longer climbing the stairs. You know that's not a safe space; it isn't what you want. Tell them you don't want to be touched or loved in this way. Don't spend time with them anymore and be among the women. Explain to the women why you want to go shopping with them, expressing the turmoil you feel when they leave you alone in their presence. Share what it's like, impatiently waiting for the sound of the car driving up; the longing to hear the gate open and safety to return. No one seems to care how you feel, and it's hard to understand why the women couldn't take you with them; surely, you're a good girl for them, too. Discuss your strengths and choices.

Don't sleep in a room alone; the temptation for prowlers is too great. Tell people how unsafe you feel when Mom goes off to play cards on the weekends. When she leaves you unattended and vulnerable, explain that you wake up in the middle of the night, no longer in your bed, and what's happening to you. Tell them you don't like it. By telling your story, you can help keep somebody else's child from waking up in a bed that's foreign to them. However, when no one comes for you, you start to wonder if they ever saw you there at all. So, I'll lie here. I'll take it. I'll hide it. One day, it'll come out. But today is not that day.

I remember hearing you explaining to Mom, trying to speak truth, but your voice was pruned. I listen to her say … 'I better not hear mother (referring to grandma) talk about this.'

When your story is met with silence, you bury it deeper. Now you feel shame, and shame often grows in silence and confusion, mixed with anger. She's added a new shadow to the secrets of men. This is manipulation, which is a form of control. It is abuse. It is a violation. Mom, not allowing you to share that secret is a way to constrain you and the narrative. Keeping that secret enabled her to keep living her life as she pleased without the responsibility to change anything. Perhaps it was her livelihood, finances, companionship, or her 'got-it-all-under-control' lifestyle.

Whatever it was she was holding on to, allowed them to violate other people, other girls just like you. Trust me, they all thought it was a secret. And you believed. This is hateful and hurtful; there is no love in it.

I know it's hard. Some days, you feel angry; others, you'll feel numb, and that's okay. Feel it; feel all of it, but don't let it define you. You may wonder "why me" more than once, that's normal. You don't have to answer that today. On many days, you'll wonder what it is that makes you special, what it is that men desire in you. What is special about you that it is

196

necessary to violate you as opposed to getting it from the women who left you behind? The women who, by lack of understanding, left you in the wolves ' den. It makes you wonder why it is more important to go where she is going and do what she is doing, rather than ensuring you are protected. It makes you wonder why she would trust other people with her precious daughter, niece, granddaughter, and cousin. It makes you wonder what is so special about you that they choose you to violate, to manipulate, and attempt to destroy you. What is it about you that they thought you were less than? That nobody cared. Nobody would believe you, nobody would trust your words, and nobody would notice the change in your demeanor. Your pain is real, but it's not your ending. Looking back on this, you'll see what is difficult has strengthened you. You'll find that it has made you resilient.

By telling your story, you will find the strength to save your own life.

I know you may be worried that someone might not like you anymore. Someone's feelings may hurt, and their daily lives may be disrupted. That's not your concern. Sometimes the truth hurts, but when it's

197

shared, healing can begin. Shout it from the rooftops, or at least the top bunk. Don't worry. I love you. I want you to be free. Be strong. Be courageous. Be bold.

You'll find that it makes you passionate about protecting other people, other young girls. You'll find that it has transformed into a source of strength. You'll find that it gave you purpose. It made you more inquisitive. You'll find that it makes you love harder. It made you much stronger in who you are. It made you determined. You realize there is life after trauma and love after pain. There is laughter after a silence. You'll see it all, and you'll feel it all. You'll enjoy all of it. You'll understand that, while this is a struggle today, it is what makes you who you are. This moment will not define your future; it will not dictate how everything else evolves. It will, however, influence everything else.

Although you don't realize it at the time, buried things don't die. They can fester and sometimes resurface later in life.

It would be 10 years later when we would face this gardening issue again… Now hidden behind a uniform on the outside, you're still bare on the inside.

Grown, trained, even armed as an active-duty Soldier—yet unprotected. The lesson of being silent has trained you that the violation goes by faster and hurts less when the secret is kept. You still believe, and it's reinforced … you are on your own. Many days, you felt God knew your name but still wondered if He was watching over you.

Predators are who they are, regardless of your age; however, they can't break you; they may have hurt you, but they didn't take your spirit. You can heal, grow, and reclaim everything stolen from you. You have the power to be more than like a rag as they used you to be.

You are not broken; you are becoming who God created you to be. We are still here, preparing to do the healing work. We will talk to God and a therapist because even in your silence, God was (is) listening.

Your story isn't just written in pain—it's recorded in divine ink, etched in heaven's memory.

You have the power to reclaim the innocence that was stolen from us. Just like a wet rag, your tears drip. But you know what … God sees and hears every one of our tears. He collects them, and you may not see what God is doing with your tears at this age, but I'm here to tell you that He will dry them up. He catches every single one. Not one tear falls unnoticed. Not one ache escapes His attention. According to Psalm 56:8 (NLT):

"You keep track of all my sorrows. You have collected all my tears in your bottle. You have recorded each one in your book."

That means your tears aren't wasted—they are witnessed, collected, and remembered. He bottles them.

Not like something to discard, but like a sacred treasure. Your tears are a testament to your journey, humanity, and endurance. He records them. Your pain is not overlooked. It's written in your life story, not just the pain but the healing that follows. God keeps a record, not to remind you of suffering, but to show how far He brings you.

He waters your growth with them. Tears may fall from grief, but water seeds of strength in time. God can use even your lowest moments to nourish your purpose. The tears from pain will grow into compassion, testimony, and ministry. He trades them for joy. Psalm 30:5 reminds us, "Weeping may endure for a night, but joy comes in the morning."

That's not just poetry, it's a promise. Your sorrow may linger for a season, but it will not define your destiny.

You will be healed, and it may not be you alone. Well, it won't be you on your own. God will heal you. Some people will believe you and stand with you, helping you recover. And that's a beautiful Black woman. It's an intelligent Black woman who other people long to be. It's a woman who knows her strength and won't let anybody take that away from her.

There are hiccups along the way because it takes time to realize your strength and realize that there is power in your tongue. You need to recognize that sharing is caring. There will be hiccups you seem ashamed of, but it's the coping mechanism you are learning now. It's where you learn to adapt so people won't see the pain. Because of the shame, you'll find that your secrets will be the choice. The silence they teach you will become the silence that strengthens you.

Remember that guilt and self-blame can linger, and they may linger for years as you try to understand why it happened to you and how they allowed it to happen. But remember to forgive yourself for whatever you thought you should have done differently.

You don't need to be perfect to be lovable, and you don't need to carry guilt that is never yours. You will be at your best with what you know, and that's enough. Your voice matters to me, and every young Black woman still figuring it out. Your story is needed, and your presence is powerful.

I want you to not focus on what is happening to you right now because you're still worthy of love, peace, and a beautiful life. You're still whole. You are still amazing. You are not what's happening to you. You are everything you choose to become.

With all the love in the world, I dare speak life over you.

You are the daughter of resilience, the granddaughter of warriors, the mother of nations, and the architect of our futures.

You will walk through fire and will not let it consume you. One day, you'll be a woman who leads—a woman who teaches. You will press on, leading others to do the same, showing compassion to those who need it, even when you long for someone to show it to you.

A woman who raises children, earns degrees, and wears a uniform with pride. You'll serve your country and community and fight for others to be seen and heard—because you know what it feels like to be invisible. You will harness that protector within, not despite the secrets and past, but because of them.

You carry the weight of being the oldest child, the only girl for so long, and seemingly, the favorite of the men. You are the example; you hold it gracefully, even when it feels too heavy. Something is divine about how you endure but let me remind you: we are not born to survive. We are made to thrive.

You'll help people find their voice because you had to fight for your own. You'll walk into rooms where your younger self wouldn't have been welcomed and take up space with your head high.

You will serve this country for 21 years in the Army, navigating spaces where you must prove yourself repeatedly and excel. You will raise three beautiful children while juggling the demands of motherhood and the military with a heart full of grit and grace. You will watch them grow into their power and be blessed with the most precious granddaughter— proof that the cycle does not have to repeat and that love can be a legacy just as much as pain.

Education is essential, so take advantage of the Army's free schooling. Earning your bachelor's degree while in uniform will help train more than 400 young recruits to become compelling storytellers. Teach them not just how to write but how to speak with courage and conviction.

As a leader, there's an opportunity to manage an office of 12 Soldiers, guiding them through personal and professional challenges—from physical fitness to financial literacy to the quiet struggles they may face building stability at home. It will be an honor to serve as the senior enlisted leader during the 9/11 crisis, helping to steady the hearts of those preparing to defend a shaken nation. To wear the uniform isn't just about duty, heart, humanity, and healing. There's pride in ensuring service members are seen, valued, and appreciated at home and abroad.

Marry a man who loves you in the way every little Black girl should grow up knowing she deserves. Travel the world. Fill your spirit with the beauty of diverse cultures and discover passion in creating spaces where women can come together, savor tea, and share wisdom.

Somewhere along the journey, you'll remember the warmth of those Monday choir-rehearsal nights—the clink of teacups, the laughter of women playing Scrabble, and the soft hum of conversation that made you feel safe, even if just for a moment. Back then, tea was the one thing children were allowed to share with the grown-ups. Coffee was reserved for

205

adulthood, but tea? Tea made space for your little hands to hold something warm, comforting, and dignified. You didn't know it then, but tea was your first invitation into sisterhood. Years later, you'll turn that memory into a mission. You'll build a business not just for yourself but for women like you who need a place to be heard, healed, and held. A business that travels because healing has no fixed address. A space where women can sit, sip, and spill the tea—freely, without judgment. Where stories are honored and voices, like yours once was, are finally heard. It's more than a tea party; it's a return to self. A reclamation. A circle of warmth where trauma meets transformation and laughter can live again. And sometimes, it starts with a cup of tea.

I encourage you to keep going.

When it doesn't look or feel good, even when the world tells you are too much. When the road is unclear and the weight of everything seems unbearable. Keep going. You are worthy of joy. You are worthy of love. You are worthy of dreams so big they scare you. And you are worthy of achieving all of them.

Do not let the pain of yesterday steal the hope of tomorrow. Do not let the voices of those who couldn't see your greatness convince you it isn't there. Walk boldly in your purpose. Do it with love, purpose, and the strength of our ancestors holding you up. Speak your truth with confidence. Love yourself deeply and without apology.

There is success in this world and a place for you in it.

You're going to laugh again. You're going to love again. And yes, you will learn to trust—slowly, carefully, but fully.

You are strong. You are brilliant. You are beautiful. You are enough.

And one day, you will look back at the girl you once were, just as I am doing now, and you will whisper to her with pride, "We made it."

We carry the spirit of those who came before us— women who loved fiercely, dreamed boldly, and fought tirelessly for a freedom I am privileged to know. Their laughter echoes in joy, their sacrifices paved the roads we now walk, and their resilience is stitched into the fabric of our being.

I think of the ones whose names I may never know but who live in our blood, pushing us to speak louder, dream bigger, and rise higher than the world said we could. Because of them, I stand here, not just as one woman but as the embodiment of generations of strength. To our great-grandmother who sang lullabies under the weight of oppression, to the neighbor who mentored young girls on porches wrapped in the summer heat, to the teacher who saw potential in a world that refused to acknowledge it—you are the threads that bind me to something greater.

Like many Black women before us, our journey has been marked by both challenges and triumphs. When you celebrate a success, listen for the whispered "well done" of generations past. Feel the weight of their hands on your back when you push through obstacles, steadying you. Each challenge you overcome is a testament to our collective power. These victories aren't ours alone—they belong to every woman who came before us and everyone who walks beside us now.

My dear, beautiful Robin,

I see you. You didn't just survive—you transformed.
With every scar, you grew stronger. With every
silence, you found a louder truth. You are the echo
of every woman who fought to be heard, the voice
of the ones still learning how. Take up space, speak
with power, love yourself fiercely, and live out loud.
The world doesn't just need your survival—it needs
your story, your joy, and your becoming. Every scar
you carry is proof that you are still here. And that is
your power. So, when you feel lost, remember this:
You are not broken. You are still becoming. And
that, too, is sacred.

You are never alone. I've got you now.

With love and unshakable faith,
Robin (Me)—the woman you survived to become

Choosing Me

By Zakiyyah Broadnax

Dear Little Me,

You've come such a long way, baby girl.

I want to hold you close right now, rock you in my arms, and whisper into your ear that you were never broken, even when everything around you tried to break you. I want to tell you that you will make it — not just survive but thrive. That the tears you cried in the dark, the ones no one saw — those tears watered your strength.

I know there were times when you thought love had to hurt. That being chosen meant sacrificing parts of yourself. That being good enough meant staying silent, being small, not rocking the boat. But love is not supposed to suffocate. It's not supposed to silence you. And it surely isn't supposed to come dressed in fear.

You were just nineteen when you left home, when you followed what you thought was love into an unfamiliar city, far from everything and everyone who had ever known your soul. After your mother was murdered by your father, at the age of 18, Toledo was supposed to be a new chapter — a

211

chance to grow, to build something with someone
you trusted. But it became something else.
Something darker.

It started slowly — the subtle shifts in the way you
were spoken to, the criticism disguised as concern,
the control hidden under the mask of "protection."
At first, you thought maybe you were imagining it.
Maybe love just wasn't what you expected. But love
isn't supposed to shrink you. And girl, you were
shrinking.

Your light — so vibrant, so powerful — started to
dim. The young woman who had dreams, who had
fought through teasing, trauma, and the
unimaginable loss of her mother, she started to
disappear. You were in a fog, day by day losing
parts of yourself.

And while you may have blamed him — and
rightfully so — I admire the way you took
responsibility for your part in it, too. You began to
see the patterns, the generational threads that had
quietly woven themselves into your life. You realized
that you were not blameless on the physical side of
things either. Domestic violence had become a

painful, repeating trend — for your mother, your sister, and now you.

But instead of hiding from that truth, you faced it. You owned it.

That's growth.
That's accountability.
That's the sign of a woman who refuses to be a victim of her own story.

For five years, you endured emotional warfare. You walked on eggshells. You questioned your worth. You stopped recognizing yourself. But you know what you didn't do? You didn't give up.

You finished nursing school. You graduated.

You crossed the stage not just for a diploma, but for your freedom. And at that moment — so many people clapped, but they had no idea what it really meant. That walk wasn't just across a platform… it was through every hardship you had to push past to get there. You weren't just handed a piece of paper — you claimed a piece of yourself.

That diploma? You used it like a key. Not just to unlock doors in the world, but to open the one that led you back home — to who you truly are. You walked away from that chapter, bruised and battered, yes, but not broken. Never broken.

You were tired — God, you were tired — but there was still something burning in you. A spark that never went out. That day gave you something more than a degree. It gave you a deep sense of accomplishment. It reminded you that you were worthy, not because of what you achieved, but because of what you overcame to achieve it. That moment reminded you that you are powerful, even when you feel small, that you're resilient, even when you feel unsure.

Back home, you tried to start fresh. You started to dream again. But sometimes, even when we try to run forward, our past follows us. And it did.

He came back.

The same man who drained your spirit, who convinced you that his love was your salvation, he returned with sweet words and apologies. And even though your gut whispered don't go back, your heart, still entangled in old memories, and feeling the connection, told you, maybe, just maybe, he meant it this time.

So, you tried again. Because Black women are taught to love hard, to endure, to hope past hope. And you loved him. Since you were sixteen, you loved him.

But he didn't change.

The betrayal cut deeper each time. The other women, the lies, the control, the gaslighting… He thought you were his and that he owned you. Each time he broke a promise, a little more of you cracked. And every time he came back with tears and vows, you tried to glue those cracks shut with forgiveness. But glue doesn't hold when the foundation is already crumbling.

He proposed. You said yes. Not because you believed in the fairytale, but because you were still holding on to the little girl who just wanted to be loved, genuinely loved. You thought maybe if you became his wife, everything would fall into place.

215

It didn't.

Marriage didn't save the relationship. It only caged you deeper.

It took you until thirty — a whole fourteen years of your life — to finally say, Enough!

And baby, when you did, you saved yourself.

That's when the healing really began.

You didn't know who you were anymore. You had been someone's partner, someone's fixer, someone's punching bag — but who were you to yourself? The journey back home was more than just physical. It was spiritual. Emotional. Soul work.

In the quiet of breaking away and the start of the need to heal, as you were slowly piecing yourself back together, something unexpected and beautiful unfolded. You met the man who would later become your second husband, your current love.

But this time, you weren't looking to be rescued. This time, you weren't trying to be completed. You were learning how to be whole on your own.

216

And in his presence, something felt different — safe, sacred, and familiar. You've always believed the two of you were connected from lifetimes ago, brought back together in this one with divine purpose.

He didn't try to fix you or shape you. Instead, he taught you something even deeper: to put yourself first without guilt, to honor your truth, no matter the cost. He reminded you that real love doesn't require self-abandonment. It encourages authenticity, even when it's uncomfortable.

With him, you learned that being loved doesn't mean losing yourself. It means being seen, fully, and still being held.

Still, healing isn't linear.

And even then, healing wasn't a straight line. It didn't unfold in perfect steps or follow some neat timeline. Some days you felt whole, other days you could barely hold yourself together.

You laughed in moments you thought you'd be crying, and you cried in moments you thought you'd be strong.

217

But that's the truth of it — healing isn't linear. It curves, it dips, it circles back. And yet, with each breath, each choice to keep going, you were still moving forward.

Fast forward to 48, approaching 50, something in you stirred. Something gentle began to rise within you — a quiet, persistent voice that had been whispering for years, but this time... I couldn't turn away. That quiet voice — the one you tried to silence with busyness and responsibilities — started to speak louder. She asked, "Who are you? Who are you without the titles, the trauma, the pain, the past? Who are you when no one's watching?"

You couldn't ignore her anymore.

So, you sat with her. You listened. You went back in time and looked at all the wounds you'd buried deep, all the lies you believed about yourself. And you made a decision that would change everything:

You chose you.

You put yourself first. You prioritized your joy, your growth, and your healing. You stopped waiting for someone to tell you that you were worthy, and you decided to believe it for yourself. You stopped hiding your scars and started showing them with pride, not because you were proud of the pain, but because you were proud that you survived it.

You fell in love with yourself.

Not the version you thought you had to be. But the real you. The woman who had walked through fire, held broken pieces of herself, and rebuilt with shaky hands. The woman who cried in silence but showed up anyway. The woman who had every reason to give up but chose to fight. You started to see her. And baby, she was beautiful.

You started doing the inner work — the hard, gritty, messy work that no one claps for. The kind of work that strips you bare and asks you to rebuild from the ground up. You faced the little girl inside you, the one who still felt abandoned, who still carried the weight of not feeling enough. You told her, "I see you. I love you. I've got you now."

And with each new day, you began to trust yourself again.

219

You created boundaries, not walls. You learned that saying no wasn't selfish — it was sacred. You gave yourself permission to rest, to breathe, to just be. And for the first time in your life, you weren't just existing — you were living.

You started pouring yourself the way you once poured into others. You pursued your passions. You built a life that honored your truth. You became a safe space for yourself — a home you could return to, no matter what.

And it showed.

In the way you walked — with your head held high, not in arrogance, but in assurance. In the way you spoke — with grace and conviction, no longer shrinking your voice to make others comfortable. In the way you loved — not out of fear of being alone, but from the overflow of your fullness.

You became everything you needed.

You started helping other women see the light in themselves, too. Because you knew what it felt like to be in the dark. You knew the ache of trying to find your way back to yourself. And now, on the other side, you extended your hand — not to save them, but to walk with them, side by side, as they saved themselves.

You became a healer, a coach, a guide — but not one who carries what isn't hers. You let go of people-pleasing, stopped shrinking to make others comfortable. Now, you lead with compassion and boundaries. That was your success. But most importantly, you became a truth-teller. Your truth. Unfiltered, unpolished, and unapologetically yours.

You turned your pain into purpose.

Every wound became a chapter. Every tear became ink. Every lesson became a message. And you started writing — not just for yourself, but for every woman who ever questioned her worth, every girl who thought she had to earn love, every soul who forgot her power.

And oh, how powerful you became.

You started businesses. You hosted events. You created spaces for women to gather, to breathe, to be seen. You reminded them of who they were. You reminded them that healing is not a destination — it's a daily choice. A journey of returning, again and again, to your truth.

Even now, at 52, you are still becoming. Still evolving. Still discovering new pieces of yourself. And that, my love, is the most beautiful part — you never stopped growing.

You've learned to dance with your imperfections. To celebrate your progress instead of punishing your pace. To give yourself the grace you once begged others to offer.

You've stopped chasing the version of success that was never meant for you — the one rooted in hustle and perfection. Instead, you've created a version of success that feels like peace. That tastes like joy. That breathes like freedom.

And you are free now.

Free from the lies. Free from the expectations. Free from the need to prove or perform. You belong to yourself, finally. Fully.

And you've never looked more radiant.

It's the glow that comes from finally knowing your worth — inside and out.

So, to the girl who thought she had to be perfect to be loved:
"You don't have to earn love by breaking yourself to fit. The right love will see you, hold you, and stay — even when you're not holding it all together."

Here's what I want to say to you, Little Me:

Thank you.

Thank you for surviving. Thank you for not giving up. Thank you for dreaming, even when it hurt. Thank you for trusting, even when you were afraid. Thank you for loving, even when it cost you everything. Thank you for being brave enough to break cycles, to say no more, to choose you.

You paved the way for me.

I carry you with me now — in every decision, every act of self-love, every boundary I set, every dream I chase. You are not just a memory. You are my foundation. My root. My beginning.

And I promise you this:

I will never abandon you again.

I will hold your hand through every storm. I will celebrate you, in every victory. I will nurture you in every season.

You are not alone anymore. You never really were. You just needed time to see that the love you were searching for was always inside you.

Here's to you — the brave, beautiful, resilient little girl who grew into a woman she could be proud of.

You made it.

And baby girl, we're just getting started.

Because life didn't stop teaching, and you didn't stop learning. You realized that healing isn't just about moving on — it's about moving differently. It's about choosing peace even when chaos is familiar. About choosing yourself, again and again, even when guilt tries to call you selfish.

You learned that some people won't clap for your growth, and that's okay. Some will miss the old version of you because they benefited from your brokenness. But you? You no longer shrink to make others feel tall. You no longer carry the weight of making everyone else comfortable at the expense of your own soul.

You started walking away from things that didn't nourish you. Conversations that felt like confrontation. Rooms that made you feel invisible. Friendships that were only loyal to your wounds, not your healing. You started saying "No more." And meaning it.

You stopped betraying yourself.

You stopped abandoning the little girl inside you every time someone else needed more of you than you had to give. You started turning inward and asking, "What do I need? What does she need?" And you listened.

And with each decision to honor yourself, you became whole.

Wholeness didn't look like perfection. It looked like choosing grace when you slipped. It looked like crying on the bathroom floor, then getting up and showing up anyway. It looked like laughing again — not because everything was perfect, but because you finally believed you deserved joy.

And let me tell you, the woman you've become — she is nothing short of a miracle.

She doesn't just walk into rooms now — she commands them. She doesn't just speak — she declares. She doesn't just dream — she builds. She knows her power. She wears it like a crown and walks in it like it's a second skin.

She is everything you prayed for.

And now, she's the one praying over others. Loving others back to life. Speaking life into broken bones and bruised spirits. She's the one who says, "I know what it feels like. You're not alone. You will rise."

You became a lighthouse.

Not because you never knew darkness, but because you remembered your way out of it.

And you're still rising.

And with each rise came deeper clarity.
Healing didn't just restore your hope — it reshaped your understanding of love.

Now love is starting to make sense — not the kind you chase, but the kind you attract when you finally come home to yourself. I learned that real love begins within. You can't expect someone else to fill a void you haven't touched. You must first learn to truly love yourself — to sit with your own heart, honor your worth, and find joy in your own presence.

Because the truth is, no one can love you better than you love yourself. Others can add to your happiness, but they can never be the source of it. And now, that's the kind of love I teach others to reach for — the kind that starts with you.

And from that place of wholeness, everything began to shift.

You stopped just surviving and started building. You're building legacies now. For your children. For your grandchildren. For every woman who thought she had to earn love by losing herself. You're rewriting narratives. You're showing up, not just for them, but for you.

And guess what?

You've forgiven yourself.

For the times you stayed too long. For the times you didn't know better. For the moments you lost yourself in the name of love. You've stopped blaming that younger version of you. She was doing the best she could with the tools she had. And now you've given her new tools — love, grace, power, truth.

You've finally realized that your past doesn't define you. It refines you.

Those broken chapters? They weren't your ending. They were your becoming. And now, with your head held high and your heart wide open, you walk boldly into every new season — not because you have all the answers, but because you finally trust yourself to figure it out.

That's the real glow-up.

Not the external. But the internal.

You healed the parts of yourself that no one clapped for. You fought silent battles and came out stronger. You faced the mirror, told the truth, and didn't look away. You became the woman you once needed.

And that's why I celebrate you.

Not just for what you've overcome, but for who you've chosen to become.

A woman rooted in truth. Wrapped in grace. Carried by the Universe. Anchored in love. A woman who lives boldly, loves deeply, and gives freely. A woman who knows her worth and no longer asks for permission to exist fully.

You are fire and water. Soft and unshakable. Gentle, yet fierce. You are divine. You are necessary. You are more than enough.

So, keep going, beautiful.

Keep becoming. Keep healing. Keep choosing you.

Because everything you've ever needed has always been inside of you.

And if you ever forget again, just come back to this letter.

Read it slowly. Let every word wrap around you like a warm blanket. Let it remind you of the truth you sometimes forget:

You are loved. You are worthy. You are whole. You are her.

With eternal love and gratitude,
Zakiyyah (Me)

Afterword

These thirteen letters closed a circle. Each writer faced what happened, named what must not repeat, and chose a steadier way to live. The pages moved by small, exact acts—truth told, help requested, limits honored, rest protected—and the result was forward motion you can trust.

Dr. Andrea "Angel" Atkinson-Taylor turned teen motherhood into legacy—education, work, service, and a family that stands upright.

Ann Marie Maloney showed how prayer and plain speech shape a life; forgiveness released weight without excusing harm.

Brandi Rhoden stayed with her inner child long enough to replace self-blame with care and to make boundaries normal, not harsh.

Charleeta Latham refused the quiet that kept abuse in place; she traded "be good and don't speak" for "be clear and be safe."

Eternity treated rest as faithful practice;

therapy and faith sat side by side without conflict.

Dr. Kim Thomas modeled discipline and partnership—study, service, and family aligned through steady choices.
Loren made joy a daily practice; anxious spirals eased when self-talk changed, and limits held.

Mauryunna Brown returned to the power of language; thoughts and words became tools for peace, not pressure.

Meisha Pon proved that asking for help is human; the armor came off and the voice came through.

Mika Dean Newton re-mothered herself; care, boundaries, and rest replaced overwork and silence.

Nikki Shantell rebuilt after violence, assault, injury, and grief; self-advocacy, therapy, and journaling marked each step.

Robin Blue named child abuse with accuracy and courage; voice became protection for her and for others.

Zakiyyah Broadnax chose herself after repeating cycles; love now means truth, not self-erasure, and community gains from that clarity.

Read together, these letters teach a few simple things: tell the truth, ask for help, keep a boundary, rest on purpose, and stay close to safe people. No theatrics. Just small choices that hold.

Harm is named, not performed. Consent stays in front. Each writer sets her own pace. Faith and therapy can share the same table. Scripture can sit next to a journal. A safety plan can sit next to a prayer. The writing is clear on purpose—steady voice, clean lines, straight attributions—so you can move through hard pages without feeling lost.

The moments are ordinary, which is why they matter: a first "no," sleeping through the night, telling a sister the truth, leaving a room that isn't safe, making an appointment, opening a notebook again. These choices work at home, at work, in church, or in court—because they are part of daily life.

The circle gets wider here. Mothers learn to re-mother themselves. Daughters grow into women who parent with new rules: safety first; honesty without cruelty; love that never asks you to erase yourself. Mentors show up in simple ways—sharing a number, offering a ride, holding a door. Quiet help counts.

If you saw yourself on these pages, take the part that fits. Keep what is private. Share only what is safe. There isn't one right way to heal or one right pace. You are allowed to start small.

Close the book with this in mind: you are not alone, you are not late, and change is allowed. Let the pages sit with you. When you're ready, try one line: "Dear Little Me, here is what I wish you knew…" Write a few sentences. Save them. That's enough for now. The rest can come in its time.

Lessons to Be Learned

(One core lesson and a few quick prompts from each author's letter)

Angel

Lesson: A setback at seventeen did not define the future; steady choices, learning, work, and love with boundaries—built a legacy.

Prompts:

- Name one early burden that forced you to grow. What skill did it teach you that still serves you?

- Write three sentences your 17-year-old self needed to hear about worth and direction.

- List the next two credentials or skills that would stabilize your family's future.

- Define "legacy" in one paragraph. What begins this month?

Ann Marie

Lesson: Plain prayer and clear speech lighten the load; forgiveness releases weight without excusing harm.

Prompts:

- Write a 5-line prayer in everyday language about one current worry.

- Finish: "Forgiving _____ means I release _____; it does **not** mean _____."

- List three places where your words need to be simpler and truer.

- Choose one person or situation and write a single sentence boundary.

Brandi

Lesson: Staying with your inner child replaces self-blame with care and makes boundaries normal.
Prompts:

- Name one childhood need. How did it shape an adult habit? What is a kinder replacement?

- Draft a boundary script you can say in under 20 words.

- Write a 6-line note to your younger self that says what no one said then.

- List two ways you will practice self-respect this week.

Charleeta

Lesson: Silence protects abuse; clarity protects people.
Prompts:

- List the silencing rules you were taught. Rewrite each as a safety rule.

- Identify one safe person. Draft a two-sentence disclosure you could share with them.

- Name a setting where you felt you had to "be good and not speak." What is today's clear line?

- Choose one practice that keeps you safe (ride home plan, check-in text, code word).

Eternity

Lesson: Rest is a faithful practice; therapy and faith can stand together.
Prompts:

- Choose a weekly rest window. Block it. Name what you will **not** do.

- Write three signs your body gives when you need to stop.

- Pair one therapy goal with one spiritual habit that supports it.

- Finish: "When I rest, I am protecting _____."

Dr. Kim

Lesson: Discipline plus partnership holds study, service, and family in place.
Prompts:

- Set one 30-day study plan (time, place, unit goal).

- Name one way your closest relationship strengthens your purpose; one way it needs support.

- Define your service lane in two sentences. Where will you show up weekly?

- Choose a keystone habit (sleep, exercise, reading). Track it for 21 days.

Loren

Lesson: Joy can be practiced; calmer self-talk and firm limits reduce spirals.
Prompts:

- Make a "joy menu" of five low-cost actions; schedule two this week.

- Reframe three anxious thoughts into grounded statements you can believe.

- Write a one-line boundary you will keep the next time you feel overloaded.

- List two people who help you return to calm. How will you ask for support?

Mauryunna

Lesson: Words shape reality; thought, body, and speech aligned bring peace; forgiveness is liberation.
Prompts:

- Write three daily declarations that start with "I am…" Keep them specific.

- Replace one harsh self-sentence with a kinder, truer one.

- Draft a short forgiveness note (to self or another): release, lesson, boundary.

- Choose one phrase you will stop saying about yourself. What replaces it?

Meisha

Lesson: Asking for help is human; when the armor comes off, the voice comes through.
Prompts:

- Text or call one person and make one specific ask today.

- List your top three supports (people, places, practices) and how to access each.

- Finish: "When I ask for help, I am honoring _____, not failing."

- Identify one place you over-perform. What will you hand back or decline?

Mika Newton

Lesson: Re-mothering yourself means giving the care, boundaries, and rest you missed.
Prompts:

- Design a 15-minute "care ritual" you can do daily (time, place, steps).

- Write a note from a Good Mother voice to you about one current stress.

- Make a "stop doing" list of three tasks that don't serve you.

- Choose one boundary that protects your sleep. Keep it for seven nights.

Nikki

Lesson: Self-advocacy, therapy, and pages on the table rebuild a life after injury, grief, and assault.
Prompts:

- Prepare a doctor's visit: one symptom summary, one timeline, three questions.

- Journal for 10 minutes on "What I wish someone had said to me then."

- List two grief rituals that help (walk, music, call, faith practice). Schedule them.

- Write a one-page safety plan: who to call, where to go, what to bring.

Robin Blue

Lesson: Naming child abuse with accuracy protects you and others; voice is protection.
Prompts:

- Map your safety net: three names, three numbers, three places.

- Draft a one-sentence disclosure you could say if needed.

- Finish: "In my family, we protect children by _____."

- Practice your voice: say out loud one truth you will not soften.

Zakiyyah

Lesson: Breaking cycles means choosing yourself and redefining love as truth plus boundaries.
Prompts:

- Define love in three lines that do not require self-erasure.

- List five early red flags you will not ignore again.

- Outline an exit plan in five steps you could follow if needed.

- Draw a small "community map": who holds you up and how to reach them fast.

One-Page Practice (use with any story)

- Write one line: **"Dear Little Me, here is what I wish you knew..."**

- Add three sentences: one truth, one boundary, one next step.

- Share it only with someone safe—or keep it for now.

- Repeat weekly for one month.

.

About The Co-Authors

Dr. Andrea "Angel" Taylor is an author, speaker, and entrepreneur, co-owner of **Soulful Sounds LLC** and founder of the **Nourish then Flourish Collective**, dedicated to inspiring healing, growth, and empowerment.

Ann-Marie Maloney is an educator, author, and coach, and founder of **Becoming Enough. Becoming You (B.E.B.Y.)**, a platform dedicated to empowering people through faith, healing, and growth.

Brandi Rhoden, licensed trauma therapist and founder of **Honeybee Wellness**, creates safe spaces for healing and empowers women to reclaim their voices, peace, and self-worth.

Charleeta Latham is a writer, poet, educator, and founder of the Birmingham chapter of **Black Girls in Art Spaces**, creating programs that foster connection, accessibility, and creativity.

Eternity Sledge, known as **Thee Multifaceted Black Girl**, is a poet, entrepreneur, and leader who blends creativity, faith, and vision to uplift others through healing and empowerment.

Dr. Kim Thomas Manning is a published writer and speaker from Plant City, FL, she shares powerful stories shaped by her journey as a mother of a child with disabilities. Dr. Kim's work focuses on healing, advocacy, and personal growth.

Loren A. Simon is a teacher, poet, and writer dedicated to fostering healing, growth, and empowerment, inspiring others through authenticity, creativity, and compassion.

Mauryunna Brown, founder of **Thee Healers Brew** and author of Pressure 44, is a creative and healing advocate who inspires others through compassion, empowerment, and self-discovery.

Meisha Pon is the founder of ***MyCircle Retreats***, Meisha inspires women to listen to their inner voice, embrace their perfectly imperfect selves, and recognize their inherent worthiness.

Mika Dean Newton, founder of **Zenmi Holistic Therapies**, is a creative and healing advocate dedicated to guiding others toward self-worth, balance, and emotional freedom.

Nikki Shantell is a writer & entrepreneur, founder of **IdentiSure: A Code 10 Company** which includes DateSure, Nikki Shantell empowers women to heal, grow, and persevere

Robin Blue is the founder of **Rendezvous N Style,** a veteran and event planner who brings discipline, creativity, and passion to every detail, helping others celebrate life with beauty, meaning, and connection.

Zakiyyah Broadnax is a writer and coach who helps women embrace self-love, set boundaries, and reclaim joy by choosing themselves and living freely without apology.

About Dear Black Woman Media

Dear Black Woman Media is a nonprofit adult education media network that centers Black women's voices. We produce learning-focused content across print, digital, audio, and live formats so readers and listeners can access clear information, practical tools, and a supportive community. Our work includes Dear Black Woman Magazine, the Dear Black Woman Podcast, the Dear Black Woman Anthology series, and chapter-led programs that highlight health, culture, business, family, and the arts.

Each publication and program follows straightforward editorial standards: verify facts, credit sources, use plain language, and offer next steps. We invite scholars, practitioners, and everyday experts to share knowledge that benefits daily life—nutrition tips, financial basics, career guidance, relationship skills, mental wellness practices, and community resources.

Membership helps sustain reporting, workshops, and chapter activities, and it includes a magazine subscription. Chapters host local meet-ups, service projects, and education sessions while the national platform connects stories and resources across cities and countries. Together, these efforts turn learning into action.

Dear Black Woman Media exists to honor lived experience, teach useful skills, and make room for healing and growth. We publish with care so that Black women worldwide can study, plan, create, lead, and pass forward what they know.

www.dearblackwomen.me

About Redd Ladys Publishing & Productions

Redd Ladys Publishing & Productions is a full-service publishing house and creative studio that supports authors from idea to marketplace. We guide projects with a clear, step-by-step process: proposal review, developmental editing, line and copy edits, proofing, interior and cover design, print and eBook formatting, ISBNs, and distribution setup. Our team prepares author assets—media kits, press releases, book trailers, and launch plans—then coordinates signings, virtual events, podcast placements, and targeted outreach.

We serve a wide range of nonfiction and select fiction: memoir, faith and wellness, education, business, cookbooks, children's titles, poetry, and anthologies. For writers who prefer assistance at the keyboard, we offer ethical ghostwriting and manuscript coaching. Transparency guides our work: clear scopes, realistic timelines, and practical budgets.

Beyond books, our production unit develops audio, video, and live programming that extend a title's reach—readings, panels, workshops, and branded series. We partner with community groups, schools, and media outlets to connect authors with readers in meaningful ways.

Redd Ladys Publishing & Productions is woman-led and U.S.-based, serving clients worldwide. Our goal is simple: help authors craft strong books, publish with excellence, and build lasting platforms that educate, inspire, and serve their audiences.

Contact Kami Redd & Co Branding for more details about our services.

About Kami Redd & Co Branding

Kami Redd Branding is a luxury brand development agency built on Kami's ReddPrint™ framework: **Refine, Execute, Design, Dominate**. The agency equips entrepreneurs, creatives, and organizations with tools to build strong, recognizable brands that align with their mission and vision. Through strategy, design, and storytelling, Kami Redd Branding helps clients position themselves for influence and long-term success. Its approach goes beyond visuals, focusing on authentic identity and purposeful execution so that brands stand out while staying true to their values.

www.kamiredd.com

Call to Action — Join the Next Volume

Who this is for

Black women ready to write a letter to your inner child and share it in the next Dear Black Woman anthology. You control what you share and your privacy (pen names welcome).

How our cohort runs (book timeline)

- **Schedule:** focused 3-month cohort starting late April each year
- **Rhythm:** daily prompts and lessons in the self-guided online portal + one live group session per month (three total)
- **Milestones:** 1st draft → edit → Final draft → publication the week before Labor Day; Crowned Legacy Pageant the following April

What you'll do

- **Write your letter (3,000–5,000 words)** — plain, honest, safe for you to write
- Follow daily online prompts
- Join the three required live sessions for guidance and steady accountability

What we provide

- Trauma-informed pacing and guardrails (consent first; no pressure for graphic detail)
- **Editorial care:** grammar, consistency, formatting—your voice stays yours
- **Self-publishing tips:** ISBN basics, layout pointers, author page setup, short launch checklist
- Contributor placement in the next volume (with author bio) + visibility across DBW platforms, including **DBW Digital Magazine**

Cost

- **Total project cost:** $650
- **Month 1 deposit:** $150 (confirms your spot)
- **Months 2–4:** $166.67 per month (3 payments = $500 total)
- **One-time option:** pay the full $650 upfront (no installments)

Optional add-on

- Custom cover + individual ISBN for your personal edition: **$375**

How to sign up (Dear Black Woman website)

1. Go to the **Dear Black Woman Anthology** page on the website
2. Click **Join / Pay Deposit** and submit the **$150** deposit
3. Complete the **Anthology Form** and review the **Co-Authors Contract**
4. Choose **Monthly (3 payments of $166.67)** or **One-Time ($650)**
5. Watch for your **welcome email** with portal access and the cohort calendar

What to bring

- A clear boundary for yourself (what you will and will not write)
- A weekly time slot you can protect
- One safe person to check in with if the work gets heavy

When you're ready to move from private words to published work, **join on the Dear Black Woman website**. Members receive a **program discount**.